Orthodoxy and Anarchism

Orthodoxy and Anarchism

Contemporary Perspectives

Edited by

Davor Džalto

LEXINGTON BOOKS/FORTRESS ACADEMIC
Lanham • Boulder • New York • London

Published by Lexington Books/Fortress Academic
Lexington Books is an imprint of The Rowman & Littlefield Publishing Group, Inc.
4501 Forbes Boulevard, Suite 200, Lanham, Maryland 20706
www.rowman.com

86-90 Paul Street, London EC2A 4NE, United Kingdom

Copyright © 2024 by The Rowman & Littlefield Publishing Group, Inc.

All rights reserved. No part of this book may be reproduced in any form or by any electronic or mechanical means, including information storage and retrieval systems, without written permission from the publisher, except by a reviewer who may quote passages in a review.

British Library Cataloguing in Publication Information Available

Library of Congress Cataloging-in-Publication Data

Names: Džalto, Davor, 1980– editor.
Title: Orthodoxy and anarchism : contemporary perspectives / edited by Davor Džalto.
Description: Lanham : Lexington Books/Fortress Academic, [2024] | Includes
  bibliographical references and index. | Summary: "This book brings together essays
  on Orthodoxy and anarchism by prominent Orthodox theologians and scholars"—
  Provided by publisher.
Identifiers: LCCN 2023045070 (print) | LCCN 2023045071 (ebook) | ISBN
  9781978715363 (cloth) | ISBN 9781978715370 (epub)
Subjects: LCSH: Christianity and politics—Orthodox Eastern Church. | Orthodox
  Eastern Church—Doctrines. | Anarchism.
Classification: LCC BX342.9.P64 O78 2024 (print) | LCC BX342.9.P64 (ebook) |
  DDC 261.7—dc23/eng/20231127
LC record available at https://lccn.loc.gov/2023045070
LC ebook record available at https://lccn.loc.gov/2023045071

♾️™ The paper used in this publication meets the minimum requirements of American
National Standard for Information Sciences—Permanence of Paper for Printed Library
Materials, ANSI/NISO Z39.48-1992.

Contents

Introduction   vii
  Davor Džalto

Chapter 1: Good News! The Son of David Is Crucified!: Anarchic
  Dimensions of the Messianic Language in the Gospel of Mark   1
  Veljko Birač

Chapter 2: "Not by Violence and Tyrannical Domination":
  Apophatic Political Theology in Gregory of Nyssa   23
  Johannes A. Steenbuch

Chapter 3: Love and Annihilation: Becoming Human in the
  Thought of St. Maximus the Confessor and Lessons from
  Contemporary Anarchism   47
  E. Brown Dewhurst

Chapter 4: Holy Foolishness as a Form of *Anarchism*   83
  Per-Arne Bodin

Chapter 5: Anarchism and Orthodoxy in Latin America   101
  Graham McGeoch

Chapter 6: Anarchy and Hierarchy: The (Nonoppressive) Holy and
  the Question of "Spiritual Aristocracy"   115
  Davor Džalto

Index   135

About the Contributors   143

Introduction

Davor Džalto

Orthodox Christianity and *anarchism* are rarely uttered in the same breath. They are usually understood as very different, if not mutually exclusive phenomena. There are many reasons for that.

One is the character of dominant political theologies in the history of Orthodox Christianity. Over the past two millennia, numerous theologians, clergymen, rulers, political philosophers, and propagandists have been constructing narratives that have rationalized the existing sociopolitical order and its power structures. Traditionally, that was some kind of monarchy. In more recent times, there is another tendency visible mostly among the theologians living in the regimes of "liberal democracy." They have been constructing theologies that rationalize, defend, and promote liberal-capitalist sociopolitical systems and their power structures (including their imperial aspirations). Many see in this a new and "progressive" kind of Orthodox political theology, compared to the traditional ("promonarchist" ones). In fact, the method in both is virtually the same: one constructs (theological) narratives that articulate, rationalize, promote, and defend the dominant political and ideological systems in which the authors of those narratives live (and from which they often benefit), whether that be the (Eastern) Roman type of government, Russian empire, or the regime of "liberal democracy" and the imperial aspirations of, say, British or American empires. In this respect, the mainstream Orthodox political theology is similar to Roman Catholic and Protestant political theologies: in all of them, as a rule, the dominant approach has been the one of a rationalization and defense of the dominant ideological and power systems, as long as they are not openly antichurch (such as the Bolshevik regime, for instance). As a result, when the dominant ideological narrative and/or political system is the one of (enlightened) absolutism, dominant theological narratives will defend and promote absolutism; when the dominant

vii

narrative and the system is the (capitalist) "liberal democratic" one, then there is an urge to rationalize and defend (capitalist) "liberal democracy" with theological arguments, and so on. The mainstream political theologies have, thus, served as more or less elaborate, more or less complex political ideologies in the service of existing political systems and their dominant power structures. Anarchist ideas have not been part of this equation.

Another reason is the character of the dominant types of anarchist philosophies. The "classical" anarchist thought was against traditional forms of religion and religious institutions, including Orthodoxy and the Orthodox Church. The reasons for this position are not difficult to grasp. They lie precisely in the alliance between dominant ideologies (including political theologies functioning as political-ideological narratives) and dominant power structures, as well as between the institution of the church and the state. This traditional bond obscured, and still obscures, many alternative tendencies in the history of Christianity, that, in the eyes of many (including most anarchists) became either completely invisible or irrelevant.

Thus, from both camps—from the camp of the dominant Orthodox political theologies/ideologies and from the camp of major anarchist philosophies—we have an exclusion of anarchist and anarchist-like tendencies in the history of Orthodoxy, which created an impression that Orthodoxy and anarchism are not only very different but also mutually incompatible concepts and phenomena. This, however, is problematic. Such a widely spread perception, from the point of view of the authors who contributed to this volume, should be revisited and should change.

The purpose of this book is to contribute to the development of a different understanding of the Orthodox tradition vis-à-vis anarchist ideas. It starts from a different presupposition, from which my book *Anarchy and the Kingdom of God* also departed—that the character of dominant political theologies in Orthodox Christianity is problematic, and it is problematic primarily from a theological point of view. The book also shows that many modern and contemporary ideas, principles, and practices that can legitimately be called *anarchist* have their parallel (sometimes also their source) in the Orthodox tradition.

The first chapter explores the anarchic dimensions of the messianic language and imagery in the Gospel of Mark. The chapter's author, Veljko Birač, argues that by using the concepts and images typical of royal power (both in the context of ancient Judaism and that of the Roman Empire), Mark effectively undermines this power, exposing it as false. Instead, the Messiah, Jesus from Nazareth, is portrayed as a "royal" figure of a different kind.

A fresh view on the relationship between anarchism, understood primarily as an active opposition to power and oppression, and patristic theology, can be seen in the second chapter in this volume, in Johannes

Introduction ix

A. Steenbuch's "'Not by Violence and Tyrannical Domination': Apophatic Political Theology in Gregory of Nyssa." Steenbuch argues that Gregory of Nyssa drew important political conclusions from his trinitarian theology, and that those political consequences remain very relevant for the major anarchist concerns (while taking into account that Gregory of Nyssa never developed a systematic political theology). Gregory's frequent criticism of political power, domination, and violence clearly expresses a sensibility to how trinitarian theology can have antiauthoritarian ramifications for how we perceive human relations, which makes it very relevant, and very compatible, with the major anarchist concerns. Not least Gregory's unprecedented criticism of the institution and practice of slavery reflects his uncompromising dedication to human freedom and equality, which Gregory saw to follow from humanity's participation in the image of God. Important is also his understanding of the Kingdom of God, which can be described as the negation of all worldly kingdoms—the Kingdom of God is freedom and love, rather than coercion and forced submission. This makes it very relevant for the anarchist approach to sociopolitical realities.

A similar approach to the patristic literature, and some of the most *iconic* theologians in the Orthodox tradition, we find in Eren Brown Dewhurst's chapter "Love and Annihilation: Becoming Human in the Thought of St Maximus the Confessor and Lessons from Contemporary Anarchism." Dewhurst explores the theology of Maximus the Confessor and its potential compatibility with the anarchist thought. Maximus' theology is focused on the transformation of the human nature which culminates in *theosis*, that is, deification. The key concepts of Maximus' theology include *logoi*, virtues, and love. Dewhurst also explores anarchist ideas and concludes that they represent an important reservoir for a theological reflection, if that reflection is built on the premise we derive from Maximus—that striving to bring the cosmos together in love is inseparably linked to the process of becoming human, while tearing the world apart, in greed and egotism, is to annihilate both oneself and the world.

In his contribution, Per-Arne Bodin takes a different approach. Instead of looking at the Orthodox patristic tradition, he focuses on one prominent phenomenon within Orthodoxy (especially in the context of Russian Orthodoxy)—the phenomenon of *holy foolishness* (*iurodstvo*). The phenomenon, Bodin claims, was always viewed with some skepticism by authorities. However, it was in the seventeenth century that both ecclesiastical and political powers became more resolute in their negative view of holy fools, seeing them as a threat, both because of their strange and unbecoming behavior, as well as because of their harsh criticism of all power. The practice, nevertheless, continued to exist even after the Russian Revolution. Bodin explores similarities between the ideas and practices that we find in *iurodstvo* and anarchism, such as the negative attitude toward power and hierarchy.

The thought of Nikolai Berdyaev, one of the greatest modern Orthodox Christian thinkers, is relevant for the last two chapters of this volume. In chapter 5, Graham McGeoch takes us to the South American context, and shows the influence that Russian anarchist ideas, and particularly those coming from the Orthodox context, had on the development of anarchist ideas in Latin America. Both anarchist ideas and Orthodoxy have been, in McGeoch's view, marginalized in the history of political and religious thought of this part of the world, where the central position has been occupied by the literature focusing on nation (state) building and the spread of liberalism, and on Roman Catholicism and, later, on the spread of Protestantism (primarily Pentecostalism). In contrast to these approaches, McGeoch sheds light on the connections between Orthodox Christianity and anarchist ideas in Latin America from the early twentieth century onward, inspiring many religious and political movements of resistance which draw on the themes of freedom.

In the last chapter of the book, in my "Anarchy and Hierarchy: The (Nonoppressive) Holy and the Question of 'Spiritual Aristocracy,'" the reader will find an analysis of anarchism, hierarchy, and the question of "spiritual aristocracy" (based on Nikolai Berdyaev). The focus is on unpacking the relationship between the liturgical, sacrifice-offering *hierophany*, and anarchism, both as a theological concept and as a method of critique of sociopolitical structures and ideologies. Anarchism is explained a method of deconstruction of power-narratives and power structures, but also as a method that allows us to go beyond the deconstruction, into a new construction, which, again, needs to be subjected to a critical examination and opposed to as soon as it becomes normative, glorified as the "best" or "ideal" model, and especially when it becomes oppressive. Anarchism as a method spares us from glorifying even the systems that would be called *anarchist*, should they be established on a larger and more permanent scale, since once established, they would also allow for establishing new power-narratives and new power structures, that an anarchist should critically examine and dismantle when the existence of these narratives and structures cannot be justified based on the principles of human freedom, dignity, and justice.

It is our wish and hope that this volume will inspire more interest both in Orthodoxy and in anarchism, and, specifically, in those obscured and marginalized narratives and approaches from the history of Orthodox theology and the Orthodox Church that, in their affirmation of freedom and in their opposition to power, oppression, and domination, can be called—*(proto)anarchist.*

Chapter 1

Good News! The Son of David Is Crucified!

Anarchic Dimensions of the Messianic Language in the Gospel of Mark

Veljko Birač

καὶ ἦν ἡ ἐπιγραφὴ τῆς αἰτίας αὐτοῦ ἐπιγεγραμμένη·
ὁ βασιλεὺς τῶν Ἰουδαίων.

Mark 15:26

INTRODUCTION

The purpose of this chapter is to explore the *anarchic* dimensions of the messiah language in the Gospel of Mark. "Anarchy" or "anarchism" represent a deconstructive approach toward the structures of power. In this case, it refers to the deconstruction and inversion of the royal ideology and the power of rules expressed in the messianic language of the Gospel of Mark.[1]

By using what will be called "deconstructive dramatic irony," the Gospel contrasts its contemporary ideologies about political rulers (Jewish and Roman) and the promised messiah of the Scriptures. The Messiah[2] of the Gospel of Mark turns the symbolism and the meaning of the political upside down. For Mark, the Messiah, Jesus from Nazareth, is a royal figure. He represents the fulfillment of ancient promises to David (2 Sam 7:12–14). This language is not unique to Mark's writing; many other "messianic" texts from

Fig. 1.1. *The King Who Would Not Be King,* ink on paper, 2023. Artist: Davor Džalto

Good News! The Son of David Is Crucified! 3

the Second Temple period share similar themes. However, he is not one of those messiahs; there is something special about this *heir of David*, the way Mark depicts him. And yet, the identity of this Messiah remains a mystery. Mark does not fully reveal it. This mystery is fortified by the tragic end of the story. The messiah—the expected *king*—shamefully dies on the cross. My argument is that it is precisely through this hidden-revealed messianic identity and the paradoxical end of the king who dies shamefully that Mark constructs a counter-narrative to the royal ideologies of both Jerusalem and Rome.

In order to show this, I will do a narrative analysis of Mark's messianic language. I first explain what it means to talk about messiah figures in the context of the Gospel of Mark and the challenges researchers face when studying this topic. I also examine specific moments in the Gospel narrative to demonstrate that Jesus, as the Messiah in Mark's text, is depicted using motifs from both the Jewish and Roman royal ideology. The analysis shows how Mark deconstructs the idealized images of rulers and their mission in the world through the way he described the trials, suffering, and crucifixion in Jerusalem. Finally, I discuss the significance of the empty tomb in the context of Mark's call to the reader to *reconstruct* the *deconstructed* messianic identity.

IN THE BEGINNING . . .
THERE WAS A MESSIANIC TEXT

The study of messianism is a well-established field, with numerous theories and approaches proposed over the past century and a half.[3] Many definitions of the meaning of the concept of "messiah" have been proposed,[4] and the typical method used is that once a researcher establishes a definition of messiah, they go then to ancient sources in search of such a figure. Thus, the problem is that there are many, and sometimes even mutually exclusive, definitions. Still, it is also challenging to define the corpus of ancient sources in which we should look for particular messianic figures that correspond to the proposed definitions.[5] Should we consider only those texts that use the term or those that describe particular messianic figures?[6] A separate question, of course, is how widespread messianic expectations were, given that our information about those expectations are often based on rare and often fragmentary texts recorded by a minority of the literate.

Despite these difficulties, a common thread can be established. All of the preserved texts about messianic figures of ancient Judaism use the Scriptural language. Whether it is the *son of David* from the Psalms of Solomon (Ps Sol 17–18) or the *Son of Man* from the Book of Enoch (1 En 37–71), the messiah for the writers of ancient Judaism always comes from the Scriptures.

Messiah, as the archaic title of the anointed kings of Jerusalem, is, following Novenson, borrowed from ancient court protocols and scripturally reinterpreted in order to say something about historical contexts in which no anointed king existed.[7] Therefore, the messiah figures in the period of the Second Temple Judaism appear as appropriations and interpretations of various concepts and images from earlier periods; for example, of Daniel's *Son of Man* (Dan 7:13–14), Isaiah's *Son of the young woman* (Is 7:14), of the *staff from the root of Jesse* (Is 11:1), the *star from Jacob* (Num 24:17), or *my Lord* (Ps 110:1). Of course, even if we accept that all of these appropriations follow similar or "same" rules (as Novenson suggests), each messianic text represents a unique exegetical expression, just as each game of chess is unique, despite all players following the same set of rules.

Following this approach, we can see that early Christian writers (Mark among them) belong to the messianic discourse of ancient Judaism.[8] Mark portrays his Messiah as part of a specific (messianic) literary corpus. As in other Second Temple messianic texts, Mark describes the Messiah as a *king* (as in 4Q458), *son of David* (as in Ps Sol 17:21), *priest* (as in 1QSa), *prophet* (as in 11Qmelch), and the so-called *eschatological superhuman* (as in 1 En 37–71), among other things. He reimagines the meaning of the archaic title by using biblical language (cf. Mk 11:9–10; 12:10–11). Mark presents his Messiah as a solution to various social, religious, and political problems.[9] And yet, the messiah language in Mark stands very much apart from most messianic discourses we find in the late Second Temple period. His Messiah is not only a scripturally reinterpreted successor of Jerusalem's throne or merely a part of the religious text. This Messiah is the central protagonist of a masterfully crafted narrative. By blending the vocabulary typical for Roman imperial ideology with the messianic discourse of Ancient Judaism, Mark introduces a new way of speaking about messiahs. Mark's redefined messianic language seeks to convey a more profound significance, an *inventive deconstruction* of the messianic discourse.[10] In order to achieve something like this, Mark employs dramatic irony.

The existence of irony in Mark is not unknown.[11] Jerry Camery-Hoggatt argues that "irony lies close to the narrative's core."[12] He also points out that Mark's irony has several levels. First, the characters in the narrative can behave or say something in an ironic tone. This level of irony is characteristic of the characters themselves. For example, during the trial in front of the high priest, Jesus is ordered to act as a prophet (Mk 14:65). From the inside of the narrative, the protagonists act ironically. They do not believe he is a prophet, and they do not expect any prophecy. Their request has a mocking purpose. However, as Camery-Hoggatt notices, there is another level of irony in Mark—dramatic, reader-oriented irony.

Good News! The Son of David Is Crucified!   5

Simply put, dramatic irony occurs when the story-line itself plays upon the reader's own repertoire of knowledge and convictions to produce a distinctive subtext. Though the reactions of the *reader* are orchestrated against that repertoire, the reactions of the story's characters cannot be. The characters are participants in the event, but they cannot know that the story about the event will be told in precisely this way.[13]

This is evident from the previous example of Mk 14:65. The *some* (τινες) and the *officers* (οἱ ὑπηρέται) of the high priest are unaware that Jesus' prophecy to Peter has been fulfilled at that very moment (cf. Mk 14:30; 65–72).[14] But the careful reader knows, and Jesus is revealed as a true prophet. Therefore, the ironic mocking of Jesus becomes (in the eyes of the reader) divine truth. This second (reader-oriented) level forces the reader to respond, take a position, and decipher anomalies.[15] Therefore, in Mark's case, it represents a perfect tool for an inventive deconstruction of the narratives about *ideal* rulers and political *saviors*.

MARK'S ROYAL MESSIAH

In Mark's story, understanding and revelation about the identity of Jesus hold great importance. Jesus, the Kingdom of God, and its mysteries are exclusively disclosed to the selected community, sometimes referred to as "those who are not outside" (Mk 4:11).[16] For everybody else in the story, he is relatively unknown. This often creates a tension between Jesus and other characters in the narrative. In other words, the knowledge about the true (messianic) identity of Jesus is something sacred and mysterious. One needs a specific context to fully understand it (cf. Mk 9:9).[17] And since the identity of Jesus is also the main component for the dramatic irony in Mark, the reader stands in the middle of everything. To fully grasp the subtle layers of the narrative, readers/listeners have to engage with the text, take a specific worldview, and respond to its message.[18] Throughout the entire narrative, it is hinted at in what way Jesus is the Messiah, but always with a dose of reserve and paradox. This slowly builds a scene for the ultimate identity question for the reader. For example, Jesus could be a prophetic bearer of the good news (cf. Mκ 1:1, 14–15), but when the question arises if he is a prophet, Peter answers: No, you are the Messiah (cf. Mκ 8:27–30). Hence, someone other than a prophet. And Jesus approves of his answer. However, it is precisely in Peter's case that Jesus shows himself as a true prophet (Mκ 14:65–72). According to a similar principle, the Messiah in Mark *is* and *is not* the expected king. The following chapter will demonstrate how Mark speaks about the royal identity of Messiah.[19]

Jesus from Nazareth—New David?

Among many roles that Jesus plays in the Gospel of Mark, his Davidssohnschaft seems the main one.[20] Although David is not mentioned by name until Mark 2:25, and Jesus is not directly identified as the "Son of David" until Mark 10:47, careful readers can notice from the beginning that the account of the Messiah is essentially a tale about the "New David." To explain the importance of the link between Jesus and David in Mark, I will focus on the following places and scenes from the Gospel: Superscription (1:1), baptismal account (1:9–11), healings/exorcisms, the triumphal entrance to Jerusalem (11:1–11), and the question about the Davidic sonship (12:35–37). It is noteworthy that all these examples associate Jesus as the anticipated savior from the lineage of David.

In the superscription (1:1), the omniscient narrator of the Gospel reveals the highest truth about Jesus' identity.[21] He is Χριστός (*Anointed One*), the promised "Son of David," somebody who rightfully can claim the throne of David. The message that constantly eludes all the other characters in the story (the true identity of Jesus) is immediately communicated to the reader. From the very beginning, the writer wants to share his omniscience with the reader as a call to observe the entire story and the fate of the main character through the prism of this first verse. Mark 1:1 makes dramatic irony possible as the reader possesses knowledge beyond that of the characters in the story.[22]

That the messianic title from the above should be understood in a Davidic context is evidenced by the description of the baptism events in Jordan (1:9–11). A few moments are essential for the Davidic identity of the Messiah. An unknown (to everyone in the story) man from Galilean town Nazareth comes, like many (see 1:5), to John for baptism. In the moment of coming out of the water, several things happen: the heavens are *torn apart, split* (σχιζομένους), the Spirit of God descends on Jesus, and god recognizes him as his son (1:10). Of these, the latter two are particularly crucial to our research. First, the Messiah is the bearer of the Spirit. In that sense, he could be understood as the *staff [and shoot] from the root of Jesse* (ῥάβδος ἐκ τῆς ῥίζης Ἰεσσαί, καὶ ἄνθος), on whom the Spirit of God *rests* (ἀναπαύω), who will establish the reign of God's peaceful Kingdom (Is 11).[23] Second, God proclaims that Messiah is his son. The allusion to 2 Sam 7:12–14 and, more importantly, Ps 2:7 is evident.[24] The Messiah of Mark represents the fulfillment of the promises God gave to David. Since Ps 2 was probably part of coronation celebrations, this scene could be understood as an anointing of the new king of Jerusalem.[25] However, the Spirit is seen only by Jesus, and the voice speaks directly to him. "He saw [εἶδεν] heavens split and dovelike Spirit . . . and the voice emerged from heaven: 'You are my son . . . ' [σὺ εἶ ὁ υἱός μου]" (Mk

Good News! The Son of David Is Crucified! 7

1:10–11). Therefore, the mysteriousness of the Messiah's identity is still preserved as the protagonists in the story are unaware of this anointing.

Another element connecting Jesus with David is his miracle-working (mainly exorcisms). More than any other Gospel, the Gospel of Mark depicts Jesus as a prominent healer. In as many as thirteen cases, the miracle healings of Jesus are narrated (+ four summaries). Of these, as many as eleven healings[26] and all four summaries (1:32–34, 39; 3:7–12; 6:53–56) are found in the first part of the Gospel (1:16–8:27). The remaining two take place on the road to Jerusalem (9:17–27; 10:46–52). Therefore, when Jesus came to Jerusalem, it is very possible to conclude that the word about him as a *prophet* (cf. later mocking in 15:65) and *healer/savior* (cf. 16:31)[27] came before him. Is there a connection between the image of Jesus as a healer and the *Son of David* messianic language? There could be.

According to the Books of Samuel (1 Sam 16:23), David is portrayed as a healer, specifically as an exorcist who can calm an *evil spirit* (τὸ πνεῦμα τὸ πονηρόν). Later interpretations speak about him as a *physician* (ἰατρός).[28] And Mark, when he talks about the deeds of the Son of David, depicts him (among other things) as a healer—primarily an exorcist.[29] His first public miracle is an exorcism (Mk 1:21–28). He is the agent of God, the bringer of the Kingdom of Peace (in contrast to the Kingdom of Satan).[30] He is on a metaphysical battlefield against the forces of evil.[31]

However, the identity of Jesus as the Messiah goes beyond his ability to perform miracles. In fact, it is during these episodes that the messianic secret is mainly emphasized. He constantly forbids the healed (or the demons he exorcizes) to proclaim him (see 1:34; 5:43, etc.). Although it is to no avail, this prohibition is significant—Jesus does not want to be known solely or primarily as a miracle worker. His ultimate purpose was to sacrifice himself for all. Therefore, understanding the Messiah as a miracle worker can only be grasped in light of the tragic end of his story.

Final examples of the royal Davidic language we find in the scene of the triumphal entrance into Jerusalem (Mk 11:1–11) and, later, in *die Davidssohnfrage* from Mk 12:35–37. These two scenes are heavy with quotations from and allusions to ancient texts, and they provide the reader with a paradoxical conclusion about the Davidic-messiah imagery.

After his preaching in Galilee and the trip to Jerusalem, Jesus enters the city while *those going before him* (οἱ προάγοντες) and *those following him* (οἱ ἀκολουθοῦντες) cry: "Blessed is he who comes in the name of the Lord! Blessed is the coming kingdom of our father David!" (Mk 11:9–10). It is interesting that Jesus, *who comes in the name of the Lord*, is associated here with *the coming kingdom of our father David*. It seems that Jesus' sermon about the coming Kingdom (Mk 1:14–15), healings, and Bartimaeus' cry

(Mk 10:47–48), formed, among his followers, an image of him as a Davidic messiah.[32] According to the story protagonists, one entering Jerusalem is undoubtedly a Davidic messiah.

However, the reader is again warned that Mark's Messiah is not "simply" the Son of David and that his identity goes beyond this designation. "How scribes say that the Messiah is the son of David? David himself said by the Holy Spirit: 'Lord said to my lord . . . ' If David himself calls him lord, then how is he [David's] son?" (Mk 12:35–37). This is the last of three direct references to Jesus as the Son of David, all of which are linked to Jerusalem and the temple.[33] In the context of this chapter, the unanswered question and the quotation from Psalm 110 (David is saying something *in the Holy Spirit*—ἐν τῷ πνεύματι τῷ ἁγίῳ) show that Mark wants to go beyond the messianic language of Ancient Judaism. The archaic title (messiah = anointed descendant of David) becomes something more (David's Lord). The true Messiah was never supposed to be merely a Son of David. The unanswered question also speaks to the readers to make their own conclusion. On top of this, it is apparent that each example from above *lacks something* in the *Davidssohnschaft* association, as Jesus goes beyond those boundaries, and his identity isn't solely based on being David's son. And the question (for Ancient Jewish context) remains: If he is not David's son, who is he?

Messiah as a Roman Emperor?

It seems that Mark is not satisfied with just one side of the royal coin. His community, after all, is not governed from Jerusalem by the *Anointed One* but rather by the *divi filius* enthroned in Rome. Therefore, somebody could assume that the salvation the Messiah prophesizes about could be identified with *Pax Romana*, established and maintained by the Roman emperor.

Scholars have noted and extensively examined the use of the Roman imperial vocabulary in Mark.[34] The Gospel is often thought to be written in the city of Rome by its Christian community, which was also its first recipient.[35] Mark employs language associated with the empire to describe God's Kingdom and Jesus as its agent or emperor.[36] In this sense, Mark expands the messianic language of ancient Judaism by importing the imperial vocabulary. This is a new moment in messianism, for even though messiahs of ancient Judaism were often portrayed as kings, no messiah in ancient Judaism was described as a new Caesar of an eternal and worldwide imperium. Mark masterfully blends these two ways of speaking, often in the same passages. The preceding examples (superscript, baptism, healings, and triumphal entrance) demonstrate this. Therefore, Mark's messianism (especially his "anarchic" and deconstructive attributes) cannot be understood without analyzing its Roman imperial dimension.

Readers are introduced to the imperial language in the superscription of the Gospel (Mk 1:1). Mark is writing a piece of literature entitled τό εὐαγγέλιον (good news), and this good news is about Jesus the Messiah (Son of God). The scriptural origin of this term is already mentioned (see note 19 of this chapter), yet there is another possible origin for it. A connection between the phrase "good news" and *Priene Calendar Inscription* has already been noticed.[37] This inscription represents an edict of the Roman provenance of Asia that aligns the provincial calendar with the Roman calendar. It also honors Augustus by making his birth year the beginning of the provincial calendar. For biblical scholars (especially those researching the New Testament), this inscription is interesting because the birth of Augustus is announced as "the beginning of the good news (τὰ εὐαγγέλια) for the world."[38] The Jewish writers were also familiar with this terminology. Josephus writes that when Vespasian became an emperor, he received "good news from Rome" (τὰ ἀπὸ τῆς Ῥώμης εὐαγγέλια).[39]

By calling his work an εὐαγγέλιον, it seems that Mark wants to offer the story of a different emperor. Given the historical context in which it was written, it could be interpreted that this gospel provides an alternative perspective to the destruction of Jerusalem by Titus and Vespasian.[40] It appears that Mark aims to present Christians with a new narrative centered around a different *divi filius*, "a counter-emperor"[41] who truly liberates, heals, promotes peace, and ultimately sacrifices himself for the redemption of his followers.

The baptismal account could be read in a similar tone. Michael Peppard noted a striking number of parallels between Mark's description of Jesus' baptism and the Roman imperial ideology that is often overlooked in the interpretation of this scene.[42] All of them seem to serve an imperial tone from the incipit. The Messiah, though unknown, is adopted by God, much like emperors Augustus and Galba.[43] In this way, he becomes worthy of being the emperor.

Another detail worth mentioning is the motif of the descending *dovelike Spirit* from Mk 1:10. Peppard finds that bird omens are a common motive in the biographies of the emperors.[44] However, Mark seems to deliberately use a dove to symbolize his counter-emperor. The dove is the opposite of the eagle, a symbol of the Roman Empire and army.[45] A nonviolent sign of fear (for Roman understanding) in Mark becomes an omen of the new (and different) emperor.

A third example of the Davidic messiahship was an image of the messiah as a healer and exorcist. We saw there that the motif of secrecy plays a significant role in this context. Jesus constantly forbids the proclamations about him as the *Son of God* (Mk 1:36), *Messiah* (8:30), or *healer* (1:43–44). Adam Winn finds that these prohibitions can be read in the light of Roman political ideology.[46] It is not unknown that some Roman emperors publicly refused to be praised (how much it was sincere and without ulterior motives is another question).[47] Therefore, Jesus's prohibitions were not necessarily perceived as strange because it is highly possible "that Mark's Roman readers would identify Jesus' behavior with the ideal behavior of their own rulers."[48] Moreover, as Margaret Froelich points out, the healing scenes (especially exorcisms) serve as a battlefield on which *legionnaire Jesus* is victorious.[49] The language in the episode with the demonized in the land of Gerasenes (Mk 5:1–20), where Jesus has power over a *legion* (5:9) of demons, complements this image.

The last example that will be analyzed is the triumphal entrance into Jerusalem. Even though the parallels between Jesus's entry into Jerusalem and the Roman triumphal processions can be drawn, Froelich argues that some crucial elements are missing in Mark's story for it to be read parallel to Roman triumph.[50] Froelich follows the suggestions of Allan T. Georgia[51] when argues that Mark's account of triumphal entry represents "the performance [that] comes before the victory, staging the eschaton for those awaiting it."[52]

From Mark 8:27, we learn that Jesus finishes his "Galilean campaign" and starts his journey to Jerusalem from Caesarea Philippi. This journey ends with a "triumphal entrance," and the "triumph" ends on the cross. Jesus is not coming to conquer the city he enters "triumphally," but rather to die in it. Both the Roman victory-triumphs dynamic (triumph after the victory) and its character are thus undermined, and its meaning inverted. The Messiah is the "king" (i.e., anti-king) who rides on a donkey to be executed in a shameful way (crucifixion). The logic of the triumph is thus inverted; a shameful defeat (death on the cross) becomes the basis for the (true) triumph of the Messiah (resurrection).

Moreover, Josephus reports that Titus gathered his armies and began his campaign on Jerusalem "from Caesarea."[53] It is highly probable that Mark's narrative reflects this campaign (and the great triumph in Rome after the destruction of Jerusalem), since the memory of Titus's conquest would have still been fresh in the minds of people at the time when Mark was writing his account. The Messiah narrative would thus offer a counter (Roman) εὐαγγέλιον, the *good news* of a "king" who marches on Jerusalem not to destroy it but "to give his life as a ransom for many" (Mk 10:45). This "campaign" and the "triumphal" entrance into Jerusalem would thus be the images of a paradoxical conquest—a "conquest" by a (self)sacrifice, out of love, which undermines violence and oppression of "worldly" emperors.

Similar to the above-analyzed instances of the superscript, baptism, and healings, the language of the empire is used almost *apophatically*. While the Messiah can be *described* using Roman imperial vocabulary, what is said is something else, precisely the opposite. His story is an εὐαγγέλιον—*good news* about an emperor who marches toward his shameful death. He is a *divi filius*, but this is hidden from the public gaze. Instead of the proud and brave eagle of the Roman legions—his omen is a dove. He is in a battle, but the battlefield is not military-political but metaphysical. He "triumphantly" marches from Caesarea to Jerusalem with the willingness to die on the cross.

The King Is Dead! Long Live the Messiah!

What is the purpose of this kind of royal messianic language? The answer is *ironically* nailed to the cross. The description of Jesus's passion occupies about half the narrative of his last week in Jerusalem (Mk 14–16). This account is heavy with allusions and quotations from different traditions. A great deal of scholarly work is done on these chapters, revealing different ideological templates for them—from the Suffering Servant of Isaiah (Is 53),[54] over the Roman triumphal processions,[55] to the death of a philosopher.[56] In order to examine the anarchic element of the royal messianic language, it is crucial to demonstrate how the passion narrative deals with the previous descriptions of the Messiah.

It has been shown that the messianic language implies both talking about the Messiah as the Son of David and the Messiah as the ideal ruler of the empire. Moreover, the whole narrative about this Messiah is centered around Jerusalem and the cross. As the narrative reaches its climax on the cross, the messianic language game also culminates with an intriguing turn. The promised king, the ideal emperor, the savior of the world—hangs on the cross. Most surprisingly, Mark says that is a good thing. That is how things should be. And the reader is invited to take a personal stand on this matter. After all, the reader knows this story is good news (Mk 1:1). The paradox about the royal identity of the Messiah starts with the trials before the Sanhedrin and Pilate and ends with Jesus' death on the cross. Through these examples, Mark radically mocks, judges, destroys, and finally reverses ancient presuppositions about political saviors, preparing the reader for the final trial of the faith—in front of the empty tomb.

On the one hand, Jesus is brought before the Sanhedrin "falsely" accused of having come to Jerusalem to destroy the Temple (like Titus) and build a new one (as the son of David).[57] But Jesus remains silent to these accusations (Mk 14:60–61) since he is neither an imperial, temple-destroying occupier nor a promised political, temple-building savior. In addition, the reader is aware that Jesus never said he was going to Jerusalem to destroy (or rebuild) the Temple; quite the contrary (see Mk 8:31; 9:31; 10:33–34). Yet, on the other hand, he is charged with blasphemy for admitting being the Messiah, the son of the Blessed One, the Heavenly Ruler, the Son of Man (see Mk 14: 61–64, Dan 7:13–14).[58]

The same thing happens before Pilate. Jesus was brought to him under the (changed) charge of being a political rebel, a pretender to the throne (Mk 15:1–14).[59] It is apparent to the reader that the accusation has been altered and that Jesus never had any aspirations for the throne. Therefore, the irony of the crucifixion of the *King of Jews* (that being a false accusation) invites the reader to rethink this aspect of the Messiah. Is he the Son of David—the King of Jews? After this, as Camery-Hoggatt noted, "Who can miss the sarcastic pathos of the cloak, or the crown of thorns, or the spittle?"[60] The entire occasion of the mocking procession looks like a distorted coronation. Messiah King was ultimately given a royal purple cloak (πορφύρα), crowned with thorns (Mk 15:17), and took his seat on the throne while the soldiers cried: *Ave Caesare!*—χαῖρε, βασιλεῦ τῶν Ἰουδαίων (Mk 15:17–18). In this twisted triumphal procession, the ideal savior of the empire is, at the same time, crowned and mocked. However, in the end, he is not (like a new Caesar) raised to the throne but to the cross, and the inscription on the cross specifies his guilt: ὁ βασιλεὺς τῶν Ἰουδαίων—the King of the Jews (Mk 15:26).

There is also an irony in the way in which this "coronation ceremony" is related to Jewish customs: the Son of David is "anointed" (enthroned) outside the Temple and outside the city.[61] As the last act of this grotesque performance, in the moment of the complete disclosure of the deepest and most sacred secrets (symbolized by the vail of the Temple being torn in two in Mk 15:38), he was, like Vespasian, proclaimed emperor—the *divi filius*, by a Roman legionnaire under the cross (Mk 15:39).

The end of the passion narrative thus meets its beginning: the reader is invited for one more time to reconsider the secret of the *good news* about Jesus, the εὐαγγέλιον about the shameful death of the Messiah, the Son of God (Χριστός, υἱός Θεοῦ, Mk 1:1). In the passion narrative, the *New David* (the ideal ruler of Israel) and the *New Caesar* (the ideal ruler of the Roman empire) expires with his last breath on the cross. Mark's narrative exposes an *anarchist* deconstruction of the traditional royal and messianic ideology.

The reader, however, is not abandoned under the cross, or in front of a sealed tomb, with only a deconstructed ideology as all that is left to them. When the preconceived notions are shattered, the reader is challenged to take the leap of faith and enter the unknown. How? Through the call to the reader to fully engage with the message of the Gospel, which appears in a brief account of what happened to the women on Sunday morning.

FAITH OF THE EMPTY TOMB

The very end of Mark leaves us in front of an empty tomb.[62] Women came to complete the burial rituals and found the empty tomb with the final message: "He is risen. He is not here" (Mk 16:6). *Young men* (νεανίσκος) in white garments instructed them to inform his disciples (including Peter) to meet him in Galilee if they believed his message. However, the women fled and remained silent (Mk 16:8–9). What kind of εὐαγγέλιον ends with the shameful death of the "king" and the silence about the empty tomb? Is the writer mocking us? "Mark's ending undercuts its beginning; it saws through the branch on which the book is perched."[63] There is no closure. The end is open.[64] Moreover, the reader (the community gathered in Jesus' name) knows that women did not stay silent. They preached, and others believed them. Otherwise, we would not have had this Gospel. Therefore, this end serves as an ideal test of faith in general, especially in the context of Jesus' messianic identity.

After the gruesome account of his trials and suffering that ended in his shameful death on the cross, readers are invited to challenge their own understandings and positions. If the reader believes in the secret revealed to him at the beginning, that Jesus is the promised Messiah, the Son of God, New David, or an ideal king, and that this Messiah, the Son of God and King died on the cross, then they must consider some questions: How is Jesus the Messiah? Why is the tomb empty? Has he indeed risen? If they have faith, the reader has to return to Galilee (that is, to the beginning of the Gospel) and read the *good news* about the death of the *Son of David and God* from the perspective of an empty tomb. Mark does not offer final solutions. The ultimate answer must be the reader's.

We can conclude that the Gospel of Mark represents an ironic narrative about royal ideology and a deconstruction of the archetypes of ideal rulers. In the ancient world, perfect emperors/kings are victors, heroes, and (demi-)gods, establishers of "eternal" kingdoms and peace. In the Gospel of Mark, Jesus is not an alternative to kings, or a better version of worldly emperors. He is an "emperor," the "ruler" of the Kingdom of God. Mark does not reject this imperial terminology. However, he ironically redefines it. Through the dramatic irony, we see a transformation, a *metamorphosis*—to use Mark's term (Mk 9:2)—of royal messianic language. We can see a transcendence from the Davidic King (earthly or eschatological) to the "king" unlike any other of that time (Jewish or Roman).

Moreover, the message of the Gospel, with its dramatic irony surrounding the King-Messiah, still remains relevant for the modern reader. Contemporary readers are also called to give a mature and responsible answer to Mark's deconstructive irony, an answer that affirms freedom. And the question prevails: Is this story not relevant in our attempt to deal with today's (self-declared) saviors of the world?

NOTES

1. The concept, thus, generally follows Davor Džalto's understanding of anarchy, as explained in Davor Džalto, *Anarchy and the Kingdom of God: From Eschatology to Orthodox Political Theology and Back* (New York: Fordham University Press, 2021).

2. Throughout this chapter, the term "Messiah" (capitalized) is only used when referring to "Mark's Messiah"—Jesus from Nazareth—since the Gospel writer identifies him as *the* Messiah. Otherwise, the term is written with a lowercase "m."

3. For the summary of the scholarly field, see Andrew Chester, "Messiah and Exaltation: Jewish Messianic and Visionary Traditions and New Testament Christology," in *Wissenschaftliche Untersuchungen Zum Neuen Testament* 207 (Tübingen: Mohr Siebeck, 2007), 205–30; Matthew V. Novenson, *The Grammar of Messianism: An Ancient Jewish Political Idiom and Its Users* (New York: Oxford University Press, 2017), 1–30.

4. For a summary of different definitions, see Chester, *Messiah and Exaltation*, 193; Novenson, *The Grammar*, 26–27.

5. Chester, *Messiah and* Exaltation, 193. See Novenson, *The Grammar*, 26–27 for the summary of different definitions.

6. John J. Collins, *The Scepter and the Star: Messianism in the Light of the Dead Sea Scrolls* (Grand Rapids, MI: Wm. B. Eerdmans Publishing Co, 2010).

7. See Novenson, *Christ among the Messiahs*, 53–63 for a more profound explanation of these rules.

8. See earlier referred list in Novenson, *Christ among the Messiahs*, 34n1 and his overall research in that study.

9. The Messiah goes beyond Israel's social and national boundaries (cf. Mk 7:24–8:10). He is ritually cleansing the Temple (Mk 11:15–17). He is engaging the taxpaying problems (Mk 12:13–17). And so on.

10. For how I use the term *deconstruction* in Mark, see a remarkable article by Stephen D. Moore, "Deconstructive Criticism: The Gospel of the Mark," in Janice Capel Anderson and Stephen D. Moore, *Mark & Method: New Approaches in Biblical Studies* (Minneapolis: Fortress Press, 1992), 84–102. Here, I follow Moore's attitude toward the nature of deconstruction influenced by Derrida's conclusion that "Deconstruction is inventive, or it is nothing at all." Jacques Derrida, "Psyche: Inventions of the Other," quoted in Moore, "Deconstructive Criticism," 99.

11. The most famous work on this topic is Jerry Camery-Hoggatt, *Irony in Mark's Gospel: Text and Subtext* (New York: Cambridge University Press, 1992). However, see also Kelly R. Iverson, "Incongruity, Humor, and Mark: Performance and Use of Laughter in the Second Gospel (Mark 8.14–21)," *New Testament Studies* 59 (December 2012): 2–19; Geoffrey David Miller, "An Intercalation Revisited: Christology, Discipleship, and Dramatic Irony in Mark 6.6b–30," *Journal for the Study of the New Testament* 35, no. 2 (2012): 176–95.

12. Camery-Hoggatt, *Irony in Mark's Gospel*, ix.

13. Ibid., 2.

Good News! The Son of David Is Crucified! 15

14. All translations in this chapter are mine (if not stated differently). For the Greek text of Mark, I follow Nestle-Aland, *Novum Testamentum Graece* (Stuttgart: Deutsche Bibelgesellschaft, 2012).

15. Camery-Hoggatt, *Irony in Mark's Gospel*, 4.

16. Reader of the Gospel also belongs to this chosen group. For more about Mark's (implied or actual) readers and their importance for the understanding of his story, see, for example, Robert M. Fowler, *Let the Reader Understand: Reader-Response Criticism and the Gospel of Mark* (Harrisburg, PA: Trinity Press International, 2001), *idem*, "Reader-Response Criticism: Figuring Mark's Reader," in Janice Capel Anderson and Stephen D. Moore, eds., *Mark and Method: New Approaches in Biblical Studies* (Minneapolis: Fortress, 2008), 59–94; David Rhoads et al., *Mark as a Story: An Introduction to the Narrative Criticism of a Gospel* (Minneapolis: Fortress, 2012), 144–46; Elizabeth Struthers Malbon, "Narrative Criticism: How Does the Story Mean?" in *In the Company of Jesus: Characters in Mark's Gospel* (Louisville, KY: Westminster John Knox, 2000), 7–9.

17. This play with the knowledge about messiah's identity (namely in Mark) is known as the messianic secret—*das Messiasgeheimnis*, a concept introduced by William Wrede. See William Wrede, *Das Messiasgeheimnis in den Evangelien; Zugleich ein Beitrag zum Verständnis des Markusevangeliums* (Göttingen: Vandenhoeck, 1901).

18. This will be shown later through concrete examples from the Gospel. About narrator-reader interconnection in Mark, see Fowler, *Let the Reader Understand*, 61–66; Rhoads et al., *Mark as a Story*, 39–43.

19. However, it is essential to remember that the royal identity is not the only characteristic of Mark's messianic language. Jesus could be understood as a prophet as well as a priest (all these attributes are categorized as messianic in Collins, *The Scepter and the Star*, 18). If we assume that the word τὸ εὐαγγέλιον (from Mk 1:1,14) originates in the LXX text of Isaiah (Is 52:7; 61:1), then Jesus represents a prophetic messenger preaching the *good news* of God. Also, throughout the Gospel narrative, Jesus foreshadows his death in Jerusalem (Mk 8:31; 9:12; 10:33–34). He tells Peter about his future betrayal (Mk 14:30). He acts as a high priest and cleanses the temple (Mk 11:15–16). And so on.

20. The title "Son of David" and the Davidic lineage of Jesus in the book of Mark have been thoroughly analyzed in biblical studies. For more about this topic, see Stephen H. Smith, "The Function of the Son of David Tradition in Mark's Gospel," *New Testament Studies* 42, no. 4 (2009): 523–39; Margaret Froelich, *Jesus and the Empire of God: Royal Language and Imperial Ideology in the Gospel of Mark*, LNTS 653 (London: T&T Clark, 2022), 44–45, 47–48; Max Botner, *Jesus Christ as the Son of David in the Gospel of Mark*, SNTSMS 174 (Cambridge: Cambridge University Press, 2019); J. Cornelis de Vos, "Messiah and Son of David in Mark 12:35–37: An Ambiguous Relationship," in Erkki Koskenniemi and David Willgren Davage, *David, Messianism, and Eschatology: Ambiguity in the Reception History of the Book of Psalms in Judaism and Christianity*, SRB 10 (Turku: Network for the Study of the Reception History of the Bible, Åbo Akademi University, 2020), 199–218.

21. For the role of the omniscient narrator in Mark, see Rhoads et al., *Mark as a Story*, 39–43.

22. See Camery-Hoggatt, *Irony in Mark's Gospel*, 93.

23. About connections between Mark's Gospel and Isaiah, see Joel Marcus, *The Way of the Lord: Christological Exegesis of the Old Testament in the Gospel of Mark* (Louisville, KY: Westminster/John Knox Press, 1992), especially chapter 2 ("Mark 1:2–3: The Gospel according to Isaiah"). For the text of Isaiah (and other LXX references) in this chapter, I use A. Rahlfs, ed., *Septuaginta: id est Vetus Testamentum graece iuxta LXX interpretes, Bd. I–II* (Stuttgart: Privileg. Württembergische Bibelanstalt, 1935).

24. See Donald Juel, *Messianic Exegesis: Christological Interpretation of the Old Testament in Early Christianity* (Minneapolis: Fortress Press, 1988), 77–88.

25. See Marcus, *The Way of the Lord*, 69–72; About the role of Ps 2 in Mark's narrative, see also Nenad Božović, "Psalm 2, 7–8 im Narrativ des Markusevangeliums," in Predrag Dragutinović, Tobias Nicklas, Kelsie G. Rodenbiker, and Vladan Tatalović, eds., *Christ of the sacred stories*, WUNT II, 453 (Tübingen: Mohr Siebeck, 2017), 325–45. Determining whether this psalm was a coronation psalm is challenging. Nevertheless, it falls under the "royal psalms" category; see Hans-Joachim Kraus, *Psalms 1–59: A Continental Commentary*, trans. Hilton C. Oswald (Minneapolis: Fortress Press, 1993), 125–26.

26. See Mk 1:21–28, 29–30, 40–45; 2:1–12; 3:1–5; 5:1–20, 21–43; 7:24–30, 31–37 with an interpolated episode in 5:25–34.

27. "He saved [ἔσωσεν] the others; he has no power to save [σῶσαι] himself." Greek verb σῴζω can mean: to save, to heal, to make whole (again), to preserve.

28. Josephus, *Ant.* 6:168, in William Whiston, trans., *The Works of Josephus: Complete and Unabridged*, new updated ed. (Peabody, MA: Hendrickson), 164. For the Greek term: https://scholarlyeditions.brill.com/reader/urn:cts:greekLit:tlg0526.tlg001 .fjo-ed1-grc:6.168 (accessed June 28, 2023).

29. Jesus is portrayed as an exorcist even when the story does not belong to the literary category of exorcism (e.g., the episode about the Syrophoenician woman). For a literary analysis of this story (and discussion to what category it belongs), see David Rhoads, *Reading Mark, Engaging the Gospel* (Minneapolis: Fortress Press, 2004), 69–73. About the title "the Holy One of God" in Mk 1:24, see Max Botner, "The Messiah Is 'the Holy One': ὁ ἅγιος τοῦ θεοῦ as a Messianic Title in Mark 1:24," *Journal of Biblical Literature* 136, no. 2 (2017): 417–33.

30. Botner, *Jesus and the Empire of God*, 36–38.

31. Ibid., 70–71.

32. It is worth noting that earlier identifying with prophets (Mk 8:28) can further enhance the Davidic image, as David was also considered a prophet, particularly in the early Christian context (cf. 2 Sam 23:2; Mk 11:36; Acts 1:16; 2:30).

33. The other two being Mark 10:46–52 and 11:9–10. See Marcus, *The Way of the Lord*, 137–39 about the connections to Jerusalem. For more about the messianic usage of Psalm 110 in Early Christianity, see Juel, *Messianic Exegesis*, 135–50; David M. Hay, *Glory at the Right Hand: Psalm 110 in Early Christianity*, SBLMS 18 (Atlanta: Society of Biblical Literature, 1989).

34. See Adam Winn, "Tyrant or Servant? Roman Political Ideology and Mark 10.42–45," *Journal for the Study of the New Testament* 36, no. 4 (2014): 325–52; and Froelich, *Jesus and the Empire of God*, and the secondary literature listed there.

35. For this chapter, the debate about the place of origin (Rome vs. Galilee) has no significance. For different arguments about the place of origin, see Winn, "Resisting Honor," 594–95 (for Roman origin), and Froelich, *Jesus and the Empire of God*, 2 (for Galilean origin).

36. Froelich, *Jesus and the Empire of God*, 32–38.

37. See Craig A. Evans, "Mark's Incipit and the Priene Calendar Inscription: From Jewish Gospel to Greco-Roman Gospel," *Journal of Greco-Roman Christianity and Judaism* 1 (2000): 67–81.

38. Cited in Evans, "Mark's Incipit and the Priene Calendar Inscription," 69, 70.

39. Josephus, *Bell.* 4:656; in Whiston, trans., *The Works of Josephus*, 695. For the Greek term: https://scholarlyeditions.brill.com/reader/urn:cts:greekLit:tlg0526.tlg004 .fjo-ed1-grc:4.656 (accessed June 28, 2023).

40. There is a general agreement among scholars that the Gospel of Mark was written around the time of the destruction of the Temple by Titus (70 CE). For the summary of the discussion about the date of origin, see Froelich, *Jesus and the Empire of God*, 2; and John S. Kloppenborg, "*Evocatio Deourum* and the Date of Mark" *Journal of Biblical Literature* 124, no. 3 (2005): 419–50.

41. Michael Peppard, "The Eagle and the Dove: Roman Imperial Sonship and the Baptism of Jesus (Mark 1.9–11)," *New Testament Studies*, 56 (2010): 431–51, 433.

42. Ibid., 433.

43. Ibid., 434–36; 438–41. Preppard's translation of the baptismal voice is quite intriguing in this sense: "You are my beloved son, whom I am pleased to choose" (note 36, p. 438).

44. Ibid., 442–45.

45. Ibid., 447.

46. Adam Winn, "Resisting Honor: The Markan Secrecy Motif and Roman Political Ideology," *Journal of Biblical Literature* 133, no. 3 (2014): 583–601.

47. See Winn's remarks on Augustus' strategy of *recusatio* in Winn, "Resisting Honor," 590–91.

48. Ibid., 595.

49. Froelich, *Jesus and the Empire of God*, 51, 71.

50. See ibid., 77.

51. Allan T. Georgia, "Translating the Triumph: Reading Mark's Crucifixion Narrative against a Roman Ritual of Power," *Journal for the Study of the New Testament* 36, no. 1 (September 2013): 17–38.

52. Froelich, *Jesus and the Empire of God*, 77–78.

53. Josephus, *Bell.* 5:40; in Whiston, trans., *The Works of Josephus*, 698. However, since there were few towns named Caesarea, it is unclear what Caesarea Joseph had in mind here. Caesarea of Philippi was also where Vespasian earlier dwelled with his legions (Josephus, *Bell.* 3:443–44; in Whiston, trans., *The Works of Josephus*, 659).

54. See Juel, *Messianic Exegesis*, 119–33; and Marcus, *The Way of the Lord*, 186–96.

55. T. E. Schmidt, "Mark 15.16–32: The Crucifixion Narrative and the Roman Triumphal Procession," *New Testament Studies* 41 (January 1995): 1–18.

56. See Helen K. Bond, "A Fitting End? Self-Denial and a Slave's Death in Mark's *Life of Jesus*," *New Testament Studies* 65, no. 4 (September 2019): 425–42.

57. The great irony of a mock trial was subtly foreshadowed from the beginning. Mark 3:6 shows that Jesus received his verdict without and before any trial. According to Camery-Hoggatt, this creates a playground for another trial—a charge of the reader against Sanhedrin. See Camery-Hoggatt, *Irony in Mark's Gospel*, 109, 174.

58. For more about the Sanhedrin's charge and later parallels with crucifixion mocking, see Adela Yarbro Collins, "The Charge of Blasphemy in Mark 14.64," *Journal for the Study of the New Testament* 26, no. 4 (2004): 379–401; and Joel F. Williams, "Foreshadowing, Echoes, and the Blasphemy at the Cross (Mark 15:29)," *Journal of Biblical Literature* 132, no. 4 (2013): 913–33.

59. Camery-Hoggatt, *Irony in Mark's Gospel*, 174–75. For the problem about Jesus' charge before Pilate, see also Justin J. Meggitt, "The Madness of King Jesus: Why Was Jesus Put to Death, but His Followers Were Not?" *Journal for the Study of the New Testament* 29, no. 4 (2007): 379–413. See also the analysis of Paula Fredriksen, "Why Was Jesus *Crucified*, but His Followers Were Not?" *Journal for the Study of the New Testament* 29, no. 4 (2007): 415–19.

60. Camery-Hoggatt, *Irony in Mark's Gospel*, 175. The entire mocking procession could be read against the Roman background. About the list of references to the triumphal processions of ancient Rome, see the remarkable work of Schmidt, "Mark 15.16–32." See also Joel Marcus, "Crucifixion as Parodic Exaltation," *Journal of Biblical Literature* 125, no. 1 (2006): 73–87.

61. About the rituals of anointing and latter messianic interpretations, see Adela Yarbro Collins and John J. Collins, *King and Messiah as Son of God: Divine, Human, and Angelic Messianic Figures in Biblical and Related Literature* (Grand Rapids, MI: Eerdmans, 2008), especially chapter 1 ("The King as Son of God").

62. It is almost a consensus that Mark's original ending was at 16:8 and that 16:9–20 was added later as an interpolation.

63. Moore, "Deconstructive Criticism," 86.

64. About the open end in Mark and the self-deconstructive nature of his work, see Moore, "Deconstructive Criticism," 86–87; and Norman R. Petersen, "When Is the End Not the End? Literary Reflections on the Ending of Mark's Narrative," *Interpretation* 34, no. 2 (1980): 151–66.

BIBLIOGRAPHY

Aland, Kurt, Barbara Aland, Johannes Karavidopoulos, Carlo M. Martini, and Bruce M. Metzger. *Novum Testamentum Graece*, 28th edition. Stuttgart: Deutsche Bibelgesellschaft, 2012.

Bond, Helen K. "A Fitting End? Self-Denial and a Slave's Death in Mark's *Life of Jesus*." *New Testament Studies* 65, no. 4 (September 2019): 425–42.

Botner, Max. *Jesus Christ as the Son of David in the Gospel of Mark*. SNTSMS 174. Cambridge: Cambridge University Press, 2019.

Botner, Max. "The Messiah Is 'the Holy One': ὁ ἅγιος τοῦ θεοῦ as a Messianic Title in Mark 1:24." *Journal of Biblical Literature* 136, no. 2 (2017): 417–33.

Božović, Nenad. "Psalm 2, 7–8 im Narrativ des Markusevangeliums." In *Christ of the Sacred Stories*, WUNT II, 453, edited by Predrag Dragutinović, Tobias Nicklas, Kelsie G. Rodenbiker, and Vladan Tatalović, 325–45. Tübingen: Mohr Siebeck, 2017.

Camery-Hoggatt, Jerry. *Irony in Mark's Gospel: Text and Subtext*. New York: Cambridge University Press, 1992.

Chester, Andrew. *Messiah and Exaltation: Jewish Messianic and Visionary Traditions and New Testament Christology. Wissenschaftliche Untersuchungen Zum Neuen Testament* 207. Tübingen: Mohr Siebeck, 2007.

Collins, John J. *The Scepter and the Star: Messianism in the Light of the Dead Sea Scrolls*. Grand Rapids, MI: Wm. B. Eerdmans Publishing Co., 2010.

Džalto, Davor. *Anarchy and the Kingdom of God: From Eschatology to Orthodox Political Theology and Back*. New York: Fordham University Press, 2021.

de Vos, J. Cornelis. "Messiah and Son of David in Mark 12:35–37: An Ambiguous Relationship." In *David, Messianism, and Eschatology: Ambiguity in the Reception History of the Book of Psalms in Judaism and Christianity*, edited by Erkki Koskenniemi and David Willgren Davage, 199–218. Turku: Network for the Study of the Reception History of the Bible, Åbo Akademi University, 2020.

Evans, Craig A. "Mark's Incipit and the Priene Calendar Inscription: From Jewish Gospel to Greco-Roman Gospel." *Journal of Greco-Roman Christianity and Judaism* 1 (2000): 67–81.

Fowler, Robert M. *Let the Reader Understand: Reader-Response Criticism and the Gospel of Mark*. Harrisburg, PA: Trinity Press International, 2001.

Fowler, Robert M. "Reader-Response Criticism: Figuring Mark's Reader." In *Mark and Method: New Approaches in Biblical Studies*, edited by Janice Capel Anderson and Stephen D. Moore, 59–94. Minneapolis: Fortress, 2008.

Fredriksen, Paula. "Why Was Jesus *Crucified*, but His Followers Were Not?" *Journal for the Study of the New Testament* 29, no. 4 (2007): 415–19.

Froelich, Margaret. *Jesus and the Empire of God: Royal Language and Imperial Ideology in the Gospel of Mark*. LNTS 653. London: T&T Clark, 2022.

Georgia, Allan T. "Translating the Triumph: Reading Mark's Crucifixion Narrative against a Roman Ritual of Power." *Journal for the Study of the New Testament* 36, no. 1 (September 2013): 17–38.

Hay, David M. *Glory at the Right Hand: Psalm 110 in Early Christianity*. SBLMS 18. Atlanta: Society of Biblical Literature, 1989.

Iverson, Kelly R. "Incongruity, Humor, and Mark: Performance and Use of Laughter in the Second Gospel (Mark 8.14–21)." *New Testament Studies* 59 (December 2012): 2–19.

Josephus. *The Works of Josephus: Complete and Unabridged*. New updated edition, translated by William Whiston. Peabody, MA: Hendrickson, 1987.

Juel, Donald. *Messianic Exegesis: Christological Interpretation of the Old Testament in Early Christianity*. Minneapolis: Fortress Press, 1988.

Kloppenborg, John S. "*Evocatio Deourum* and the Date of Mark." *Journal of Biblical Literature* 124, no. 3 (2005): 419–50.

Kraus, Hans-Joachim. *Psalms 1–59: A Continental Commentary*, translated by Hilton C. Oswald. Minneapolis: Fortress Press, 1993.

Malbon, Elizabeth Struthers. *In the Company of Jesus: Characters in Mark's Gospel*. Louisville, KY: Westminster John Knox, 2000.

Marcus, Joel. "Crucifixion as Parodic Exaltation." *Journal of Biblical Literature* 125, no. 1 (2006): 73–87.

———. *The Way of the Lord: Christological Exegesis of the Old Testament in the Gospel of Mark*. Louisville, KY: Westminster/John Knox Press, 1992.

Meggitt, Justin J. "The Madness of King Jesus: Why Was Jesus Put to Death, but His Followers Were Not?" *Journal for the Study of the New Testament* 29, no. 4 (2007): 379–413.

Miller, Geoffrey David. "An Intercalation Revisited: Christology, Discipleship, and Dramatic Irony in Mark 6.6b–30." *Journal for the Study of the New Testament* 35, no. 2 (2012): 176–95.

Moore, Stephen D. "Deconstructive Criticism: The Gospel of the Mark." In *Mark & Method: New Approaches in Biblical Studies*, edited by Janice Capel Anderson and Stephen D. Moore, 84–102. Minneapolis: Fortress Press, 1992.

Novenson, Matthew V. *The Grammar of Messianism: An Ancient Jewish Political Idiom and Its Users*. New York: Oxford University Press, 2017.

Novenson, Matthew V. *Christ among the Messiahs: Christ Language in Paul and Messiah Language in Ancient Judaism*. New York: Oxford University Press, 2012.

Peppard, Michael. "The Eagle and the Dove: Roman Imperial Sonship and the Baptism of Jesus (Mark 1.9–11)." *New Testament Studies* 56 (2010): 431–51.

Petersen, Norman R. "When Is the End Not the End? Literary Reflections on the Ending of Mark's Narrative." *Interpretation* 34, no. 2 (1980): 151–66.

Rahlfs, A., ed. *Septuaginta: id est Vetus Testamentum graece iuxta LXX interpretes, Bd. I–II*. Stuttgart: Privileg. Württembergische Bibelanstalt, 1935.

Rhoads, David. *Reading Mark, Engaging the Gospel*. Minneapolis: Fortress Press, 2004.

Rhoads, David et al. *Mark as a Story: An Introduction to the Narrative Criticism of a Gospel*. Minneapolis: Fortress, 2012.

Schmidt, T. E. "Mark 15.16–32: The Crucifixion Narrative and the Roman Triumphal Procession." *New Testament Studies* 41 (January 1995): 1–18.

Smith, Stephen H. "The Function of the Son of David Tradition in Mark's Gospel." *New Testament Studies* 42, no. 4 (2009): 523–39.

Williams, Joel F. "Foreshadowing, Echoes, and the Blasphemy at the Cross (Mark 15:29)." *Journal of Biblical Literature* 132, no. 4 (2013): 913–33.

Winn, Adam. "Resisting Honor: The Markan Secrecy Motif and Roman Political Ideology." *Journal of Biblical Literature* 133, no. 3 (2014): 583–601.

———. "Tyrant or Servant? Roman Political Ideology and Mark 10.42–45." *Journal for the Study of the New Testament* 36, no. 4 (2014): 325–52.

Wrede, William. *Das Messiasgeheimnis in den Evangelien; Zugleich ein Beitrag zum Verständnis des Markusevangeliums.* Göttingen: Vandenhoeck, 1901.
Yarbro Collins, Adela. "The Charge of Blasphemy in Mark 14.64." *Journal for the Study of the New Testament* 26, no. 4 (2004): 379–401.
Yarbro Collins, Adela, and John J. Collins. *King and Messiah as Son of God: Divine, Human, and Angelic Messianic Figures in Biblical and Related Literature.* Grand Rapids, MI: Eerdmans, 2008.

Chapter 2

"Not by Violence and Tyrannical Domination"

Apophatic Political Theology in Gregory of Nyssa

Johannes A. Steenbuch

When the Russian philosopher Nicolai Berdyaev (1874–1948) famously argued that "the Kingdom of God is anarchy" he added that this was "a truth of apophatic theology," and that the "religious truth of anarchism is a truth of apophatics."[1] By doing so Berdyaev associated his definition of anarchy as freedom from power and domination with a strong theological current that can be traced back to the first centuries of Christian thinking. Among the most important exponents of this tradition was Gregory of Nyssa, who is still venerated today by Eastern Orthodox churches as well as Roman Catholics and many Protestants. A growing interest in the theology of early Christianity in recent years has made Gregory and his fellow Cappadocians a much favored go-to in discussions on trinitarian orthodoxy, as well as in matters of Christian ethics and moral philosophy.

Gregory of Nyssa (c. 335–395) was a bishop in the province of Cappadocia in what is now Turkey. Being among the most important Christian thinkers of the fourth century, Gregory is famous for his defense of trinitarian orthodoxy. His thinking is characterized by a highly apophatic approach to theology that does not seek to define the divine nature in positive terms, but only speaks using negations of what God is not. However, Gregory was also the author of a great amount of moral philosophical and spiritual writings and sermons. In many cases these exhibit a critical attitude toward political power and domination. While this may seem peripheral in comparison to central subjects such

Fig. 2.1. *Not by Violence (Gregory of Nyssa)*, ink on paper, 2023. Artist: Davor Džalto

as trinitarian and apophatic theology, Gregory's criticism of political power is deeply rooted in his core theological convictions.

Many of Gregory's most explicit texts in this regard, such as his sermons on the Beatitudes and Ecclesiastes, were probably penned during or after he was exiled by the emperor Valens from 376 to 378.[2] Gregory may have been responding to what he experienced as unjust treatment, but his writings should also be considered in the wider political and religious context of the fourth century. Following what is sometimes dubbed the "Constantinian turn," Christianity became a still more important political factor after the Edict of Milan in 313. In 381 the decrees of Theodosius I made Christianity the official religion of the Roman Empire. Before that, Gregory participated in the council in Constantinople in 380, and as a bishop he must have been in touch with the political power games that were the cruder side of the theoretical discussions on theological orthodoxy. This only makes his criticism of power and domination more surprising. What is perhaps most striking is that Gregory's firm and often very explicit denunciation of political power was not just made in philosophical writings directed at a small, intellectual audience. Rather, some of his most ardent attacks on power and domination were made in sermons that may potentially have reached the ears of the very objects of his criticism.

Being a bishop himself, Gregory was not free from participating in hierarchy and order, but if we are to take the words of his brother Basil for granted, Gregory's "simplicity" made him almost unfit for exercising ecclesial authority in his small diocese.[3] Gregory's suspicion of domination and the exercise of power was not just rooted in the traits of his personal character, however, but also firmly in theological and philosophical convictions. Even if he did not develop what we today would consider a systematic political theology, the fact that Gregory seems to have based his views on power and domination on his deeper theological convictions should lead to a consideration of how classical trinitarian orthodoxy is not, in fact, politically or ethically neutral, but was seen to have important moral philosophical implications by those who defended it.

Those who today make a claim to classical trinitarian orthodoxy should at least be ready to acknowledge that what we may call a strong "anarchic impulse" flows from the Nicene doctrine of the trinity as it was perceived by theologians like Gregory of Nyssa. By this I mean an appreciation of the equality of humans made in the image of the triune God together with a critical attitude to all forms of power and violence in human relations. Of course, Gregory and his fellow Cappadocians were not "anarchists" in the modern sense, but the frequent emphasis on human dignity, freedom, and equality does have consequences for political theology.[4] The question then is: How

26   *Johannes A. Steenbuch*

does classical trinitarian theology have practical consequences through a critical attitude to political power and domination?

AGAINST SUBORDINATIONISM

It may not seem obvious how speculative theological questions such as those related to trinitarian theology can have any practical bearings. One of the great philosophers of the eighteenth century, Immanuel Kant, famously argued that absolutely nothing worthwhile for the practical life can be made out of the doctrine of the trinity.[5] Late antique Christians like Gregory of Nyssa would have disagreed. In fact, for Gregory theology and ethics were intrinsically linked, as will be shown in the following.

As a result of controversies over the divinity of Christ, the Nicene creed had been formulated in 325 to make it clear that the Son is of the same nature or essence as the Father. During the fourth century controversies continued, however, with much political impact. After the death of Constantine in 337, shifting emperors sided with non-nicenes who held that the Son is to some degree subordinate to the Father. Gregory, who was exiled from 376 to 378 during the reign of Valens, became personally involved in this controversy together with his brother Basil, both writing important works defending the essential equality of the divine persons. Basil and Gregory rejected the claim that the Son was subordinate to the Father. Instead they affirmed that all three persons of the trinity are equally God. While some of the arguments for trinitarian orthodoxy are highly philosophical, involving sophisticated theories of language, some of Gregory's arguments also have an explicit bearing on political theology.

In his book *Against Eunomius*, Gregory argued that if the Son is created then his lordship over creation must imply that a part of creation has been made ruler over the rest of creation.[6] If the Son is created, then the Lord of all things has not inherited his status as Lord from his divine nature, but from an unjust division of created nature. Only if the Son is superior in nature to created humans, can he be Lord. It amounts to a kind of usurpation, says Gregory, to divide a creation that is "of equal value in nature" (homotimô tês fyseôs) into slaves and a ruling power, "as if, as the result of an arbitrary distribution, these same privileges had been piled at random on one who after that distribution got preferred to his equals."[7] Humanity has received dominion over animals because of its rational nature, which the animals do not have, but if Christ was a creature he would not be essentially different to humans, and as such would not have the right to his lordship over humanity.

Gregory goes on to argue in this context that human governments experience "such frequent revolutions" due to the fact that "it is impracticable that those who have equal value by nature should be excluded from power," as he puts it.[8] Notice that Gregory is, in fact, not here making an explicitly normative claim, but is simply saying that it would be against the order of nature if a created rational being was made lord over other created rational beings. The point is that since we affirm that Christ is indeed Lord, we must also affirm that he is uncreated, if we are not to take his lordship to be illegitimate. The implicit normative premises of this argument are, however, quite easily discerned. Although Gregory is making a point about the relations in the trinity and the trinity's relation to creation, he obviously has a lot to say about human relations in the process as well. Saying that Christ only has the right to rule over human beings because he is himself God, as argued by Gregory against subordinationism, seems to be equal to saying that human persons, not being God, do not have this right.

There is also a more positive side to the argument. In order to illustrate how God can be meaningfully said to be three persons in one substance, Gregory and his brother Basil frequently made use of what is sometimes called the social analogy. To put it in short, just as humanity is made up of a multitude of persons with a common human nature, God consists of three persons with a common divine nature. This line of reasoning is present in Gregory's writings against Eunomius, where he argues that the Father and the Son share the same divine being similar to how all humans are fully human.[9] For example, Silvanus and Timothy are listed after Paul in Scripture, but obviously this does not make them less human, says Gregory, since number is a matter of sequence rather than being or nature.

The argument reappears in Gregory's letter to Ablabius on trinitarian theology. If the social analogy was not to result in a too loose conception of the divine nature, as if the unity of the divine persons was only nominal and not ontological, Gregory needed to emphasize the ontological unity of human nature. In his letter Gregory goes as far as arguing that it is a "customary abuse of language" to refer in the plural to those who are not divided in nature.[10] Even though we can refer to particular persons by separating them from the multitude, this should not be taken to mean that each human person has an individual nature that can be separated from the rest. In fact, humanity is, says Gregory, "an absolutely indivisible unit" that cannot be separated or divided with the individuals who participate in it.[11]

It should come as no surprise if this has consequences for how we perceive human relations. The basis for the analogy between God and humanity is the notion from Genesis 1:27 that humans have been created in (or according to, *kat'*) the image of God.[12] This makes every human being infinitely valuable as all reflect the divine goodness. The importance of this notion for anthropology was affirmed by many early Christian writers, but Gregory in particular emphasizes how it is humanity as such, rather than just humans considered as individuals, that is made in the divine image. The consequences for social ethics seems clear: If God consists in three equal persons, then the relations of the human persons that make up humanity should in some way reflect the equality among the divine persons.

APOPHATIC POLITICAL THEOLOGY?

As already suggested, basic to Gregory's theology was a sharp distinction between creation and the uncreated nature of God. In this he was drawing on a fundamental idea in classical Christian theology as it evolved from the first centuries and onward. What has sometimes been described as "the Christian distinction between God and everything else"[13] was central to the apophatic or negative theology developed by authors such as Justin Martyr and Clement of Alexandria, who emphasized the ineffability and incomprehensibility of the divine nature. Gregory equally affirmed the radical gap (*diastema*) that naturally persists between creator and creation.[14] This gap means that God can only be described indirectly, either by describing God's activities or relations, or by negative definitions of what God is not. As Gregory says in his polemics against Eunomius, "the created and uncreated are as diametrically opposed to each other as their names are."[15] Such apophatic theology is, in fact, a necessary corollary to trinitarian theology. When we name God as Father or Son we are not describing the divine essence, but only the relations that persist between the divine persons.

Together with trinitarian non-subordinationism, the Christian distinction between God and creation has implications for political theology. If God is radically different from creation, then God is not some sort of first principle in a hierarchy of principles. The trinity is not a hierarchy reaching down from heaven to earth, but an egalitarian community of the divine persons that, being itself infinite in nature, at the same time defines the boundaries of finite, created nature. As Gregory puts it in his catechetical oration, all creation is of "equal value" to God since all creation is "equally removed" from the unapproachable divine nature.[16]

That this distinction between God and human beings does indeed have political implications becomes clear in Gregory's first sermon on the Beatitudes. Here he argues against the pretensions of rulers to have power over human life and death: "Those whose offices cause them to parade on the stage of life [. . .] remain no longer within human limits," remarks Gregory in a critical tone, "but intrude themselves into the authority of Divine power," "believing themselves to be masters" (*kyrioi*) "over life and death."[17] This attack may arguably have come off as particularly offensive, as it was explicitly directed at a prideful young ruler. It is not clear whether Gregory is addressing an actual ruler or just a fictional one, but his critical remarks on power (*arche*) seems easily applicable to the exercise of offices in general. As Gregory argues elsewhere, titles are no more than titles from which "no superiority over the subordinate" accrues.[18] Hierarchy is, in other words, only nominal, not essential. In this way, negative theology puts a limit to created beings' attempts at usurping divine power.

The apophatic conception of God seems to imply that political principles must at least partly be derived negatively from theology, as limits to political power rather than positive affirmations of some neatly defined order of power. While risking anachronism, such an approach could perhaps be described as a "negative political theology" or "apophatic political theology."[19] This is, of course, not to say that trinitarian orthodoxy via apophatic theology leads to a political preference for anarchy in the sense of disorder. As Gregory of Nazianzus argued, disorder follows from atheism and polytheism, since both lack a single governing principle as the one we find in monotheism. The trinitarian kind of monotheism is not, however, defined as "the sovereignty of a single person," but as "the single rule produced by equality of nature, harmony of will."[20] Something similar is going on when Gregory of Nyssa argued that Christ only has the right to rule over creation because he is equal in nature to God the Father, as described above.

THE (UN-)KINGDOM OF GOD

The apophatic approach to theology is arguably a part of the background for Gregory's remarks on the Kingdom of God in his third sermon on *Our Lord's Prayer*.[21] When we pray for the coming of the Kingdom of God, we pray to be delivered from the reign and tyranny of death and evil, says Gregory, but we are not praying that death and evil will be substituted for just another kingdom in the usual sense of certain power relations. God is indeed all-powerful, but he does not rule through force and violence: "There is one true and perfect power which is above all things and governs the whole universe," says Gregory, but "it rules not by violence and tyrannical dictatorship, which enforces the obedience of its subjects through fear and compulsion."[22] It is only to ease communication that the Kingdom of Heaven is called a Kingdom. In other words, while there might be some analogical likeness between what we call a "kingdom" and the Kingdom of God, the two are quite unlike in that the Kingdom of God does not involve force and domination. The Kingdom of God is not a definite political order, but a spiritual reality that only has an analogical likeness to worldly kingdoms.

In one of the sermons on the beatitudes, Gregory emphasizes that when Jesus says that "the Kingdom of God is within you" (Luke 17:21), the point

30   *Johannes A. Steenbuch*

is that although "the inaccessible light of God" cannot be directly seen, the Kingdom of God can be perceived indirectly in the soul, as the sun in a mirror, when we purge all evil from our hearts by love and right living.[23] It is not possible for human beings to ascend to the Kingdom of Heaven by their own means, but it is possible to negate evils such as hate, greed, and violence that keeps us from entering the Kingdom. This somewhat apophatic approach to the Kingdom of God could perhaps be developed in terms of what Mark Van Steenwyk has called "the Unkingdom of God."[24] While it cannot be reduced to a set of positive definitions and ideals, the Kingdom of God may be described as the negation of the power and domination that characterizes worldly kingdoms.

This is where Nicolai Berdyaev's claim about the apophatic truth in anarchism becomes relevant again. Berdyaev defined anarchy as a state of freedom and the absence of power of humans over each other.[25] This freedom can only be defined in negative (or apophatic) definitions, as it must be derived from the freedom of God in which humans share. While Gregory does not define the Kingdom of God as "anarchy," he is quite emphatic, like Berdyaev, in making it clear that the Kingdom of God does not consist in power and domination, but in freedom.

REDEFINING JUSTICE

Gregory's apophatic idea of the Kingdom of God also seems to be implicit in his conception of justice. Since justice is a name for God, who is by nature ineffable and incomprehensible, justice cannot be defined in positive terms, but must be defined as the negation of injustice rather than as something definable on its own terms.[26] This also suggests that, since God is infinite, justice, being a name for God, is always more than what can be grasped in finite terms of, for example, law.[27] Justice is God himself, not some order of power.

This approach comes to full fruition in Gregory's deconstruction of worldly concepts of justice in his fourth sermon on the beatitudes. Here Gregory discusses Jesus' saying that "blessed are they that hunger and thirst for justice, for they shall have their fill" (Matt 5:6). What is justice? To begin with, Gregory considers the definition of justice according to "the words of those outside." By this he properly means those standard philosophical accounts that define justice as a matter of equal distribution of either goods, punishment, or praise in accordance with desert.[28] This definition of justice is to a large degree a matter of ruling fairly. However, argues Gregory, justice cannot be a matter of ruling (*archein*) in a certain way, since the inequality of life makes it clear that most people would then have no chances of being just. Since the superiority of some over others logically implies inequality, most people do not have the opportunity to rule in a just way, thus being incapable of participating in justice according to this definition.

It is not completely clear whether Gregory is attempting to point out a performative contradiction by arguing that equal distribution requires inequality, or whether he is simply saying that it is unfair to exclude most people from the possibility of being just. While the former reading would be more "anarchistic," the latter reading seems to be the more "democratic" option. Perhaps he is arguing both, but at any rate, in Gregory's mind justice cannot simply be a matter of ruling in a certain way. In his sermon on justice, Gregory ends up rejecting the notion that considers justice to be an intrinsic property or even a virtue of the human person. True justice is, in fact, nothing but God the Word himself: "[I]t seems to me," says Gregory, "that through the ideas of virtue and justice the Lord proposes Himself to the desire of His hearers."[29] This, however, also means that justice cannot be a property of human relations in and of themselves.

According to this "bolder interpretation" of justice, as Gregory describes it, they who hunger and thirst for justice are simply the ones who hunger and thirst for the Lord, who "became for us wisdom from God, justification, sanctification and redemption, but also Bread descending from Heaven and living water."[30] Though presented as "bold," this claim is not without precursors. Origen famously argued that Jesus Christ is himself the Kingdom of God (*autobasileia*), implying that participation in the Kingdom is identical to participation in the life of Christ himself. While not explicitly identifying Jesus with the Kingdom of God, Gregory, who had high views of Origen, seems to be saying something similar about justice. Justice is not a matter of certain political states of affairs, but a matter of participation in, or communion with, God's justice through a relation to the Word.

It could be argued that Gregory ends up legitimizing inequality if justice is not a matter of equal distribution. Such claims are often associated with individualistic forms of piety that sees righteousness as a matter of inward faith rather than living in accordance with certain social ethical standards. However, this arguably misses the point. Gregory is not saying that equal distribution is irrelevant for justice, but rather that justice infinitely transcends all accounts of possibly just political states of affairs. As we learn from apophatic theology, there is always more to say.

FREEDOM AND ANTHROPOLOGY

Gregory's theological anthropology is not just expressed in his high view on the equal dignity of human persons, but also in apophatically tinged notions of human freedom.[31] Humanity, being made in the image of God, reflects the

32 *Johannes A. Steenbuch*

unity of the divine persons in one shared nature. Moreover, in accordance with apophatic theology, human nature simultaneously reflects the ineffability and incomprehensibility of God.[32] It is exactly by being incomprehensible that the human soul reflects its divine archetype. As Gregory puts it in his anthropological treatise *On the Making of Man*, "since the nature of our mind, which is the likeness of the Creator, evades our knowledge, it has an accurate resemblance to the superior nature."[33]

For this reason, humans are always more than what can be grasped by external descriptions. While human persons, like the divine persons, can be described by their relations, human nature as such transcends every description. In this way, Gregory's anthropology may perhaps be described as "anti-essentialistic."[34] Human persons are, in other words, always infinitely more than what they seem to be at first sight. We should learn to distinguish between ourselves and what surrounds us, urges Gregory in his commentary to the *Song of Songs*.[35] Freedom is achieved when we do not identify too closely with our external characteristics, but are assimilated to God who is the ineffable essence of rational freedom. Holiness is not a matter of complying with a set of norms, but of imitating the ineffable divine nature.

In the dialogue *On the Soul and the Resurrection*, Gregory's sister Macrina defines "liberty" (eleutheria) in Platonic terms as a state where the human person is "self-regulating" (*autokratés*) and without a master (*adespoton*).[36] What can seem paradoxical to the modern reader is how this freedom or liberty is not ontologically independent of, or contrary to, God's freedom. Think, for example, of Louis Auguste Blanqui's famous slogan, "No God, no master!" or Michail Bakunin, who argued that the idea of God as master logically implies that humans must be slaves.[37] However, for Macrina and Gregory having God as master is exactly what makes it possible for human persons to be free and autonomous. This is because human freedom is nothing in itself but only something in relation to God's freedom. Humans are free to the degree that they participate in the freedom of God.

Human freedom must, then, be derived from its ontological source in God. The divine being is the fountain of all virtue, says Macrina, which is why true liberty is only possible when God is made "all in all." This is an important point in the Cappadocian interpretation of the passage in the Epistle to the Corinthians, where Paul famously argues that the end will come when everything has been submitted to the Son, who will then submit his kingdom to the Father, so that God can be "all in all" (1 Cor. 15:20–28). Gregory agreed, and argued that submission to God does not mean a slave-like enforced submission against one's will, but a freely willed union with God that in turn makes it possible to partake in the freedom of God.[38] While Christ can be said to submit himself and his kingdom to the Father, this does not mean that the second person of the trinity becomes subordinated to its first person after

"Not by Violence and Tyrannical Domination" 33

all, but that the subjection of humanity to God happens through the work of Christ on our behalf. Subjection to God is not "some sort of servile humility," says Gregory, but "our subjection consists of a kingdom, incorruptibility and blessedness living in us."[39]

This again explains how Gregory can conceive of the Kingdom of God as something quite different from worldly kingdoms. Assimilation to God does not mean blind submission to an alien will, but the participation in God's freedom that makes human autonomy possible in the first place.

GREGORY'S CRITICISM OF SLAVERY

It should be clear by now how Gregory understood human dignity through the lens of trinitarian orthodoxy together with his apophatic theology. That this has consequences for social ethics becomes clearest, perhaps, in Gregory's famous attack on the institution of slavery. While others before him had advocated for a more humane treatment of slaves, Gregory may have been the first to explicitly denounce the institution of slavery itself on principal grounds.[40] This happens in one of his sermons on Ecclesiastes, where Gregory discusses the admission of the Ecclesiast to have bought "male and female slaves" (Eccl. 2:7). Gregory's reaction is unequivocally critical: "What!?," cries Gregory abruptly, "you condemn a human, a free and self-ruling creature to slavery, and legislate against God by ignoring his law for nature!".[41] To be precise, it is a matter of divine legislation that human nature must be considered free (*eleuthera*) and self-ruling (*autexousion*). In other words, slavery goes against natural law.

Gregory goes on to explain that humanity as such, having been made in the image of God, has been made the ruler (*arche*) of the earth, something which is also inalienably true for the person made a slave: "The one made on the specific terms that he should be the owner of the earth, and appointed to government by the Creator—him you bring under the yoke of slavery, as though defying and fighting against the divine decree."[42] Every human person has been made ruler of the earth, but dividing up human persons in categories of master and slave is—the point seems to be—absurd: "by dividing the human species in two with 'slavery' and 'ownership' you have caused it to be enslaved to itself, and to be the owner of itself."[43] The point is not just that it is wrong to divide humanity, but rather that humanity can in fact not be divided even if individuals are subjected to slavery. There is an almost "Kantian" flavor to this argument: The whole of humanity is present in every human being made in the image of God, which is why human nature cannot be divided into two without logical contradiction.

34   *Johannes A. Steenbuch*

Gregory adds that everything on earth belongs to every human person, since everyone equally participates in the humanity that has been created to rule in common. However, since buying a person also implies buying that person's property, buying a human person implies buying everything on earth: "the property of the person sold is bound to be sold with him," says Gregory, but "how much do we think the whole earth is worth?"[44] In other words, if everything belongs to every single person, then there is nothing left in the world that can buy that person together with that person's property. While the argument may seem far-fetched, Gregory's point is simply that no price is high enough to pay for the human soul and everything that goes with it, but also that the exercise of power implied in slavery cannot but result in contradictions against the law of nature.

In addition to this somewhat anthropological side of the argument there is, just as important, an argument derived from soteriology. Since humanity has been made in the image of God, only God has the right to make humanity a slave, says Gregory, but he surprisingly quickly goes on to add that this right belongs "not even to God himself."[45] This is because God has set humanity free once and for all through the death and resurrection of Christ. The gospel reiterates human freedom. As argued above, that God is master and lord does not imply that humans are slaves, since Christ by his incarnation, death and resurrection has made it possible to participate in God's freedom. This is an important soteriological perspective with eschatological ramifications that will be considered again below. First a few more considerations on property and the virtue of sharing.

Property Is Theft!

An important point in Gregory's sermon on slavery is that humanity is created to possess the earth in common. This puts new light on Gregory's consider-ations on justice and the distribution of wealth. Even if justice is not first of all a matter of equal distribution, as described above, true justice neverthe-less implies a necessary consideration for equal distribution. This is because humanity participates in common in Christ. While justice is Christ himself, participation in Christ produces a concern for equality and sharing.[46]

This becomes clear when we return to Gregory's sermons on the Lord's Prayer. When we pray to God for bread, we do not "ask Him for landed estates, or military commands, or political leadership" or "a prominent posi-tion in assemblies," says Gregory, but "only bread!"[47] If God is justice itself, this means that "anyone who procures food for themselves through covetous-ness cannot have his bread from God." The "bread of God," says Gregory, is "above all the fruit of justice."[48] While justice may not in itself be a matter of equal distribution, but of participation in the Word of God, this participation

"*Not by Violence and Tyrannical Domination*" 35

necessarily implies a concern for the needs of others. Since Christ is justice, taking on the name of a Christian means participating in the justice of Christ, argues Gregory elsewhere, which also means to feed the hungry, loving one's neighbor, and so on.[49]

The abundance of the rich is not only wrong in itself, but the cause of "two illnesses contrary to one another," says Gregory in a sermon on good works: "your excess of satiety and your brother's hunger."[50] All good belongs to God who is the Good itself, but this also means that we should put limits to our wealth and let "a part of your possession belong to the poor."[51] It should come as no surprise, then, if Gregory like his contemporary Christians did not share the modern idea of absolute property rights.[52] The Cappadocians may themselves have been wealthy landowners, but they show a clear concern about the need to share with the poor.[53] Gregory's brother Basil asked in a sermon, "Who are the robbers? Those who take for themselves what rightfully belongs to everyone," and famously concluded that "the clothes you store in your cupboard belongs to the poor."[54] John Chrysostom agreed and defined theft as not sharing one's riches with the poor.[55]

It could be argued that the virtue ethics often associated with late antique and medieval Christian theology is overtly individualistic due to its focus on the piety of the individual soul, but the above suggests that the accounts of virtue in Gregory's sermons should be seen in a larger ethical framework. For example, when Gregory criticizes the pursuit of riches in his sermons on Ecclesiastes, at face value this sounds like a standard argument against inordinate desires for material things: "This is human life," says Gregory, "ambition is sand, power is sand, wealth is sand, and sand each of the pleasures eagerly enjoyed in the flesh."[56] In the kind of virtue ethics that was common among Christians, only love for God brings any lasting satisfaction, while love for material things does not, since material things are transient and perishable. Gregory's criticism of the pursuit for wealth and power is, however, not only based on this conception of individual virtue and piety as was clear from Gregory's sermon on slavery.

In this sermon Gregory also addresses and criticizes the excessive and meaningless exploitation of natural resources, such as gold. While this may seem unrelated to his criticism of slavery, the point again seems to be that greed not only distorts our relation to nature, when nature is instrumentalized and made into mere resources, but it also distorts our relations to others as was the case with slavery. Gregory considers the objection that it is harmless to gather riches "from the mines of the earth," but he then draws attention to the fact that Ecclesiastes also talks about "the peculiar treasure of kings and of the countries."[57] These, observes Gregory, are collected from the subjects of royal power using force and violence. Even if gathering riches was in itself harmless, this use of violence and power makes procuring riches a sin. The

36 *Johannes A. Steenbuch*

pursuit of wealth cannot be isolated from human relations that become distorted by the ambitions of the powerful. Individual virtue cannot be separated from social ethics.

THE DISEASE OF LOVE OF RULE

Virtue can be understood as the exercise of rational freedom that requires not being subject to irrational passions (the ideal of *apatheia*). When we fail to exercise our rational freedom, we become subject to irrational impulses. This understanding of sin can seem individualistic at first sight, with its focus on the psychology of the individual soul, but for Gregory the result of failing to exercise one's rational freedom is a distortion of human relations: "Most people do not judge for themselves how things are by nature," argues Gregory, but instead they look to "the customs of their forebears" and make irrational habits their criterion of the good.[58] As a consequence, people "thrust themselves into positions of authority" (*árchas*) and "power" (*dynasteía*) and make much of prominence in this world and material things. Following customs rather than reason results, in other words, in perverted notions of power and authority.

The desire to rule over others, though closely related to greed, is not just a sin among others. The desire to rule is in fact the root cause of sin. Gregory, in his catechetical oration, explains how the Devil "begot in himself the darkness of vice, and became sick with love of power, the beginning of the inclination to the worse and the mother, as it were, of the rest of vice."[59] In other words, "the disease of love of rule,"[60] as an older translation puts it, may be defined as the "original sin" *per se* to the degree that this Latin notion is applicable to Gregory's theology at all. At any rate, this perspective on sin is reminiscent of Augustine's definition of pride as the cardinal sin in which the first humans sought to gain self-sufficiency by becoming like God with dire political ramifications: "Pride hates a fellowship of equality under God, and wishes to impose its own dominion upon its equals, in place of God's rule," wrote Augustine in his *City of God*, a generation after Gregory.[61] Gregory's definition of sin as resulting from "the disease of love of rule" captures well these political aspects of sin as a kind of pride.

Domination and violence is, however, not only the product of pride, but pride is also produced by power. The foundation of pride "is usually high office and the power that goes with it," says Gregory in his sermon on humility.[62] Gregory does not seem to have shared Augustine's political realism, where some sort of order of domination is necessary and as such just after the fall in order to curb the consequences of sin. While never denying the need for order in society, Gregory does not seem to moderate his principled criticism of domination and power. This could, of course, be explained by the context of writing. Augustine saw the need for a strong political power to uphold the crumbling Empire, while Gregory had perhaps lived a somewhat peaceful life in Cappadocia until being exiled by political power. Gregory may not have experienced the authorities as a source of peace, but rather as a source of disorder. Gregory is not saying that all political offices and order are evil or bad, but he is quite explicit in rejecting the violence and domination that they produce.

CURING THE DISEASE BY
HUMILITY AND PEACEMAKING

It is easy to criticize power and property, but what is the alternative? Is it possible at all to have human relations not stained by domination and inequality? How do we cure the "disease of love of rule"? Such questions seem especially urgent in ideological environments where the exercise of power is often seen to be inevitable. Are not all human relationships per definition perfused by power and domination? We should not be surprised if Gregory would emphatically reject the underlying premises of this question. Domination and inequality of power is not an inherent and unavoidable part of nature, but an expression of sin and evil.

In accordance with the (by then) traditional definition of evil as privation, Gregory understands evil as resulting from the sinful turning away of creatures from their source in God. If the mother of all sin is the "disease of love of rule" then the cure for Gregory is, not surprisingly, a return to God. It is not possible, however, to imitate the divine nature as such, Gregory argues in his sermon on humility. Instead we must imitate God as revealed in Christ.[63] It is, in other words, not God as sovereign and king that is to be our ethical role model, but God as servant, Jesus, who, though being king, became a poor servant for us (2 Cor. 8:9; Phil. 2:7). Gregory explains that since "the sense of superiority" is ingrained in most human persons, Jesus makes the eviction of pride from our character the starting-point of his beatitudes. It is significant that humility is here understood in political terms. If the young ruler, criticized by Gregory, would just look to the example of Jesus and become poor in spirit, he would learn to observe the "equal respect" we owe to the members of the human race. Becoming poor in spirit, he will "not exalt himself impertinently against his own race (*to homogenes*) on account of that deceptive show of office (*archên tragôdian*)."[64] Gregory is not saying that the young ruler attacked in his sermon should quit his office, but he does establish some quite clear limits for the exercise of political power. Perhaps more importantly, Gregory calls for alternatives to power and domination.

38 *Johannes A. Steenbuch*

Humility does not mean a helpless dependence on God's sovereign power, but implies a restoration of the freedom and autonomy that humanity was created with in the first place. This is the first step in replacing power and domination with the equality and freedom that comes from participating in God. In the subsequent sermons on the beatitudes, Gregory would explain in further detail how humans could become children of God. There continues to be an apophatic element in this, as in the case of peacemaking. The opposite of love, says Gregory, is hate, anger, rage, envy, hypocrisy, and the calamity of war, while peace obliterates these evils by its very presence.[65] Peace is reached through the negation of these things. A peacemaker is someone who eliminates the "disease" of envy that produces murder, and unites the members of humanity by banishing the evils of human nature.[66] Obviously, that the good is in some sense reached through the negation of evil should not be confused with the idea that violence and destruction are necessary for the creation of positive goods. Rather, what is to be negated is negativity itself, so to speak. The Christian is not, in other words, supposed to violently destroy the order of society, but is rather to engage in alternatives to violence and domination.

In this way, by its use of negative definitions for the good, apophatic theology plays an ethical role as a tool for achieving a state of freedom by banishing the disease of love of rule from the human soul. The negation of unequal power relations, domination and violence in the pursuance of their opposites, is a part of the apophatic engagement with the Kingdom of God that is free of these things.

ESCHATOLOGY AND THE ROLE OF THE CHURCH

David Bentley Hart has pointed out, in an essay on Gregory of Nyssa, that his anthropology can only be fully appreciated in relation to his eschatology.[67] If this is true, eschatology should also be considered in the present context. Gregory's views differ from the later Augustinian idea of an eternal separation of the elect few from the mass of damnation. According to this view, a state of universal equality and freedom may have been the original intention of creation, but having forfeited its original purposes, humanity will have to do with an eternal division between the few saved and the unsaved majority. Such division, however, is not possible in Gregory's mind, recalling that humanity is not simply the sum of individuals, but an indivisible unity. Not only is humanity created in the image of God, but humanity is also in the process of being restored to its original state of freedom, equality and harmony.

While recent attempts have been made at explaining away Gregory's seemingly clear support for the doctrine of the restoration of all things (the

"Not by Violence and Tyrannical Domination"   39

apokatastasis pantôn), these typically focus narrowly on ambiguous statements made by Gregory in his catechetical oration.[68] However, in his commentary on Paul's epistle to the Corinthians 15:20–28, Gregory is more clear. Here he argues that "none of the beings that have come to existence thanks to God will fall out of the Kingdom of God, when every evilness [. . .] have been consumed by the fusion of the purifying fire."[69] While some are already here and now voluntarily united to God, others will have to go through a state of purgation in order to be set free from the dominion of sin and death. At any rate, the purpose is the final restoration of the freedom and equality that humanity was intended to enjoy in the first place.

As already pointed out in the above, the subjection to the Kingdom of God does not mean a servile or forced submission, but a freely willed union with God in which the subject is paradoxically made a partaker of the autonomy of God, thus becoming a fully free and autonomous person in the self-same act of submission. It was obvious for Gregory, of course, that this freedom is still lacking for most people. Even if God has once and for all set humanity free, as emphasized in the sermon on slavery, most people are not, in fact, free from sin and irrational passions like pride. Inequality and domination is still very real. Salvation is in principle achieved by the works of Christ in his death and resurrection, but salvation is only realized when people come to partake in the new humanity. This new humanity is proclaimed in the community that is the Church.

In his commentary on the *Song of Songs*, Gregory explains that the Church is the order (*kosmos*) in which the "manifold wisdom of God" is made manifest (cf. Eph. 3:10). By the witness of the Church it can be perceived how Christ became a servant while remaining king, and how "the power of the adversary" was overcome by "the weakness of the cross."[70] In accordance with his nonviolent theory of the atonement, Gregory sees Jesus' death and resurrection as the role model for a nonviolent way of life. What has sometimes been described as the "ransom theory of the atonement" should not, in the case of Gregory, be considered simply in terms of a forensic transaction between God and the Devil, but is rather a matter of how God overcomes power and domination by weakness and nonviolent love. God's wisdom is "multiform" as it does not overcome evil with evil, or violence with violence, but on the contrary overcomes evil with good.[71] The atonement makes it clear that God is fundamentally adverse to violence and domination. The Church is the new creation where this attitude to power and domination is made manifest, not just through the preaching of the gospel, but perhaps even more so through the practices of the community of Christians. In other words, the Church is the anarchic community where the Kingdom of God is present in anticipation of the future restoration of humanity to its original state of equality and rational freedom.

This perspective arguably challenges contemporary individualistic notions of faith. We may often be prone to think that the opposite of hierarchy and inequality must be individual liberty. Such liberal conceptions, however, often overlook the fact that liberty and community are in fact intrinsically related. This is also why the Church, as the community of those who here and now live in accordance with the Kingdom of God, is more than just the sum of the individuals that make up the Church. The Kingdom of God is not only a matter of individual piety. Neither is it just another version of the cliché that the gospel is about changing hearts, not politics. There is no real change of heart, no true submission to the Kingdom of God, if this does not play out in social relations. Christianity, says Gregory, can simply be defined as the imitation of the divine nature, but this imitation takes place in the life of the Church, whose members serve each other rather than rule over each other.[72] In doing this, they witness in practice to how God has in principle restored human relations by overcoming the power of sin and death.

Perceiving the Church as the locus of Christian ethics does not mean that Christian ethics do not have an impact on the wider society. Gregory's emphatic criticism of political power and domination is of a principled nature, and as such applicable to the practices of Christian and non-Christian societies alike. It is equally true, however, that the theological premises of Gregory's arguments mean that his criticism cannot be simply translated into secular terms without seriously distorting the argument. Anyone interested in making use of Gregory's ideas should arguably avoid the double temptation of either withdrawal or accepting the secular premises of the public discourse. The Church should bear a universal witness to the freedom and equal value of all persons belonging to humanity—not in order to exercise power over the public discourse, but on the contrary, to be a witness to the Kingdom of God that is "anarchy."

NOTES

1. Nicolai Berdyaev, *Slavery and Freedom* (New York: Charles Scribner's, 1944), 147–48. Berdyaev was critical of anarchism as a political ideology and movement, but nevertheless acknowledged the "religious truth" of anarchism. Berdyaev had high view of Gregory, who in Berdyaev's mind was the Church Father that came closest to defining a true Christian anthropology.

2. For the dating of Gregory's works, see Raphael A. Cadenhead, "Appendix: The Chronology of Gregory's Oeuvre," in *The Body and Desire: Gregory of Nyssa's Ascetical Theology* (Berkeley: University of California Press, 2018), 163ff.

"Not by Violence and Tyrannical Domination" 41

3. *Ep.* 100; Basil of Caesarea, "Letter 100," in *Nicene and Post-Nicene Fathers, Second Series, vol. 8.*, ed. P. Schaff and H. Wace (Buffalo, NY: Christian Literature Publishing Co., 1895), 184.

4. See also Johannes Aakjær Steenbuch, "A Christian Anarchist? Gregory of Nyssa's Criticism of Political Power," *Political Theology* 17, no. 6 (2016): 573–88.

5. Kant, "Der Streit der Fakultäten," in *Werke in zehn Bänden, vol. 9*, ed. Wilhelm Weischedel (Darmstadt: Wiss Buchges, 1983), 303.

6. *Con. Eun.* 1.1.527–528; Gregory of Nyssa, *Against Eunomius*, in *Nicene and Post-Nicene Fathers, Second Series, vol. 5*, ed. P. Schaff and H. Wace (Buffalo, NY: Christian Literature Publishing Co., 1893), 84.

7. Ibid., my translation.

8. Ibid., my translation.

9. *Con. Eun.* 1.1.173–174; *Con. Eun.* 1.1.202–203; Gregory of Nyssa, *Against Eunomius*, 52–56.

10. Ibid. Gregory is, of course, making a point about how the Greek language of his time was used, but a similar point could be made when talking about "human beings" rather than simply "human being" in English. For this reason I have chosen to stick with "humans." An alternative may be "human persons."

11. Ibid. See also Giulio Maspero, *Trinity and Man: Gregory of Nyssa's Ad Ablabium* (Leiden: Brill, 2007).

12. See especially *De Op. Hom.*; Gregory of Nyssa, *On the Making of Man*, in *Nicene and Post-Nicene Fathers, Second Series, vol. 5*, ed. P. Schaff and H. Wace (Buffalo, NY: Christian Literature Publishing Co., 1893).

13. Robert Sokolowski, *The God of Faith and Reason: Foundations of Christian Theology* (Washington, DC: CUA Press, 1995).

14. *Con. Eun.* 2.1.69; Gregory of Nyssa, *Against Eunomius*, 257. Scot Douglass, *Theology of the Gap: Cappadocian Language Theory and the Trinitarian Controversy* (New York: Peter Lang, 2005).

15. *Con. Eun.* 1.1.504; Gregory of Nyssa, *Against Eunomius*, 81. In the words of Hans Uhrs von Balthasar, the primary characteristic of creation is for Gregory that it is not God. See Hans Uhrs von Balthasar, *Presence and Thought: Essay on the Religious Philosophy of Gregory of Nyssa* (San Francisco: Ignatius Press, 1995), 27.

16. *Or. Cat.* 27.4; Gregory of Nyssa, *Catechetical Discourse—A Handbook for Catechists by St. Gregory of Nyssa*, trans. Ignatius Green (New York: St Vladimirs Seminary Press, 2019), 122.

17. *De Beat.* PG 44.1205; Gregory of Nyssa, "The Beatitudes," in *The Lord's Prayer, the Beatitudes*, trans. H.C. Graef (New York: Paulist Press, 1953), 94.

18. Gregory of Nyssa, "Homily 4 on Ecclesiastes," 75.

19. I borrow this concept from Jacob Taubes. See Martin Terpstra and Theo de Wit, "'No Spiritual Investment in the World as It Is': Jacob Taubes's Negative Political Theology," in *Flight of the Gods: Philosophical Perspectives on Negative Theology*, ed. Ilse N. Bulhof and Laurens ten Kate (Kampen: Kok Agora, 2000), 319–53.

20. *De fil.* 2; Gregory of Nazianzus, "Oration 29," in *On God and Christ: The Five Theological Orations and Two Letters to Cledonius*, trans. F. Williams and L. Wickham (New York: St Vladimir's Seminary Press, 2002), 70.

42   *Johannes A. Steenbuch*

21. Gregory of Nyssa, "The Lord's Prayer," 51.

22. Ibid.

23. Ibid.

24. Mark van Steenwyk, *The Unkingdom of God: Embracing the Subversive Power of Repentance* (Westmont, IL: IVP Books, 2013).

25. Berdyaev, *Slavery and Freedom*, 147–48.

26. *Con. Eun.* 2.1.132; Gregory of Nyssa, *Against Eunomius*, 263.

27. As Jacques Derrida famously puts it, justice is not the law since justice exceeds law and calculation. Jacques Derrida, "Force of Law: The 'Mystical Foundations of Authority,'" in *Deconstruction and the Possibility of Justice*, ed. D. Cornell, M. Rosenfeld, and D. Carlson (London: Routledge, 1992).

28. *De Beat.* PG 44.1236; Gregory of Nyssa, "The Beatitudes," 120.

29. *De Beat.* PG. 44.1245; Gregory of Nyssa, "The Beatitudes," 128.

30. Ibid.

31. Gregory joined other early Christians who agreed on the importance of the freedom of the human will, often against Gnostics who held some sort of predestination, or against the Pagan beliefs in astral determinism. See George Karamanolis, *The Philosophy of Early Christianity* (New York: Routledge, 2013), 144.

32. Gregory unfolds this thought many times, but perhaps most strikingly in *De Op. Hom.* 9,2; Gregory of Nyssa, "On the Making of Man," 396.

33. Ibid.

34. Not, of course, in the sense that humans do not have an "essence," but in the sense that the human essence cannot be defined. This is also why such things as sexual properties do not belong to the essence of human persons as illustrated by Gregory's biography of his sister Macrina who has transcended sexual properties. *Vita s. Mac.* 6–9; Gregory of Nyssa, *The Life of Saint Macrina*, trans. Kevin Corrigan (Eugene, OR: Wipf & Stock, 2005), 21. This is arguably what makes it possible for Macrina to hold the role of a teacher to Gregory in the celebrated dialogue *On the Soul and the Resurrection.* See also Anna Silvas, *Macrina the Younger, Philosopher of God* (Turnhout: Brepols, 2008), 110.

35. *In Cant.* 63; Gregory of Nyssa, *Homilies on the Song of Songs*, 71.

36. *De An. et Res.* 101–5; Gregory of Nyssa, "On the Soul and the Resurrection," in *Nicene and Post-Nicene Fathers, Second Series, vol. 5*, ed. P. Schaff and H. Wace (Buffalo, NY: Christian Literature Publishing Co., 1893), 452.

37. Michail Bakunin, *God and the State* (New York: Dover Publications, 1970 [1872].

38. *In Illud* 27–28; Gregory of Nyssa, "When (the Father) Will Subject All Things to (the Son), Then (the Son) Himself Will Be Subjected to Him (the Father) Who Subjects All Things to Him (the Son). A Treatise on First Corinthians 15.28," trans. Casimir McCambley, in Greek Orthodox Theological Review 28 (1983), 1–25. See also Basil the Great, *Commentary on the Prophet Isaiah*, trans. Nikolai A. Lipatov (University of Birmingham, 1997), 275–76.

39. *In Illud* 27–28. Gregory of Nyssa, "When (the Father) Will Subject All Things to (the Son)." Gregory of Nazianzus makes a similar point. See Gregory of Nazianzus, "Oration 30," 96. The idea in recent evangelical theology of an "eternal

functional subordination" in the trinity cannot be supported by Cappadocian theology, since the submission of Christ is only a submission of Christ's human nature on part of humanity. See, e.g., Matthew L. Tinkham, "Neo-Subordinationism: The Alien Argumentation in the Gender Debate," in *Andrews University Seminary Studies* 5, no. 2 (2017): 237–90.

40. See Ilaria Ramelli, *Social Justice and the Legitimacy of Slavery* (Oxford: Oxford University Press, 2016), 172ff; Karamanolis, *The Philosophy of Early Christianity*, 235; Hans Boersma, *Embodiment and Virtue in Gregory of Nyssa: An Anagogical Approach* (Oxford: Oxford University Press, 2013), 147ff; Trevor Dennis, "Man Beyond Price: Gregory of Nyssa and Slavery," in *Heaven and Earth: Essex Essays in Theology and Ethics*, ed. Andrew Linzey and Peter Wexler (Worthing: Churchman Publishing Ltd., 1986).

41. *In Eccl.* 335.11, my translation; Gregory of Nyssa, "Homily 4 on Ecclesiastes," in *International Colloquium on Gregory of Nyssa. Gregory of Nyssa, Homilies on Ecclesiastes: An English Version with Supporting Studies: Proceedings of the Seventh International Colloquium on Gregory of Nyssa*, ed. S.G. Hall (Berlin, New York: W. de Gruyter, 1993), 73.

42. Ibid.

43. *In Eccl.* 335.11; Gregory of Nyssa, "Homily 4 on Ecclesiastes," 74.

44. Ibid.

45. Ibid.

46. This line of thinking can be found already in Clement of Alexandria, who argued that the ownership of natural resources is communal since all humans participate in the same divine Logos. *Paed.* 2.12.120.3–6; Clement of Alexandria, *Christ the Educator (The Fathers of the Church, vol. 23)* (Washington, DC: CUA Press, 2010), 192.

47. Gregory of Nyssa, "The Lord's Prayer," 63–64.

48. Ibid., 67.

49. *Prof.* 133, 15–20; Gregory of Nyssa, *Ascetical Works (The Fathers of the Church, vol. 5 8)*, trans. V.W. Callahan (Washington, DC: CUA Press, 1999), 85.

50. *De Benef,* 96–97. Quoted from Ramelli, *Social Justice and the Legitimacy of Slavery*, 200.

51. *De Benef,* 101–03. Quoted from Ramelli, *Social Justice and the Legitimacy of Slavery*, 201.

52. Ilaria Ramilli observes that for Gregory, "the surplus" of the rich "is in fact stolen from the poor" and is therefore an evil possession." Ramelli, *Social Justice and the Legitimacy of Slavery*, 192.

53. See Justo L. Gonzalez, *Faith and Wealth: A History of Early Christian Ideas on the Origin, Significance, and Use of Money* (Eugene, OR: Wipf and Stock Publishers, 2002), 183.

54. Basil, "I Will Tear Down My Barns," in *On Social Justice*, trans. P. Schroeber (New York: St Vladimir's Seminary Press, 2009), 69–70.

55. See Charles Avila, *Ownership: Early Christian Teaching* (Eugene, OR: Wipf and Stock Publishers, 2004), 82–85.

56. *In Eccl.* 290.7; Gregory of Nyssa, "Homily 1 on Ecclesiastes," in *International Colloquium on Gregory of Nyssa*, 41.

57. *In Eccl.* 339.12; Gregory of Nyssa, "Homily 4 on Ecclesiastes," 76.

58. *In Cant.* 65; Gregory of Nyssa, *Homilies on the Song of Songs*, trans. R.A. Norris (Atlanta: Society of Biblical Literature, 2012), 73.

59. *Or. Cat.* 23.1; Gregory of Nyssa, *Catechetical Discourse*, 111.

60. Gregory of Nyssa, *The Great Catechism*, in *Nicene and Post-Nicene Fathers, Second Series, vol. 5*, ed. P. Schaff and H. Wace (Buffalo, NY: Christian Literature Publishing Co., 1893), 493.

61. *De Civ. Dei* 19,12; Augustine, *The City of God against the Pagans*, trans. R.W. Dyson (Cambridge: Cambridge University Press, 1998), 936.

62. Gregory of Nyssa, "The Beatitudes," 93.

63. Ibid., 90.

64. Ibid., 95.

65. Ibid., 159.

66. Ibid., 164.

67. David Bentley Hart, "The Whole of Humanity: Gregory of Nyssa's Critique of Slavery in Light of His Eschatology," in *The Hidden and the Manifest: Essays in Theology and Metaphysics* (Grand Rapids, MI: Wm. B. Eerdmans Publishing Co., 2017), 237–53.

68. See, e.g., Ignatius Green, "Introduction," in Gregory of Nyssa, *Catechetical Discourse*, 38ff. Cf. Ilaria Ramelli, *The Christian Doctrine of Apokatastasis* (Leiden: Brill, 2013), 372ff.

69. *In Illud* 14,21; Quoted from Ramelli, *The Christian Doctrine of Apoktastasis*, 412.

70. *In Cant.* 255; Gregory of Nyssa, *Homilies on the Song of Songs*, 269.

71. See Johannes Aakjær Steenbuch, "The Multiform Wisdom of God, Apophasis and the Church in Gregory of Nyssa's Reading of Rom 1.20 in Cant XIII," in *Gregory of Nyssa: In Canticum Canticorum: Analytical and Supporting Studies. Proceedings of the 13th International Colloquium on Gregory of Nyssa, Vigiliae Christianae, Supplements, vol. 150*, ed. G. Maspero, M. Brugarolas, and I. Vigarelli (Leiden: Brill, 2018).

72. *Prof.* 133,15–20; Gregory of Nyssa, *Ascetical Works*, 85.

BIBLIOGRAPHY

Augustine. *The City of God against the Pagans*. Translated by R.W. Dyson. Cambridge: Cambridge University Press, 1998.

Avila, Charles. *Ownership: Early Christian Teaching*. Eugene, OR: Wipf and Stock Publishers, 2004.

Bakunin, Michail. *God and the State*. New York: Dover Publications, 1970.

Balthasar, Hans Uhrs von. *Presence and Thought: Essay on the Religious Philosophy of Gregory of Nyssa*. San Francisco: Ignatius Press, 1995.

"Not by Violence and Tyrannical Domination" 45

Basil. *Commentary on the Prophet Isaiah.* Translated by Nikolai A. Lipatov. University of Birmingham, 1997.

———. "I Will Tear Down My Barns." In *On Social Justice.* Translated by P. Schroeber. New York: St Vladimir's Seminary Press, 2009.

Berdyaev, Nicolai. *Slavery and Freedom.* New York: Charles Scribner's, 1944.

Boersma, Hans. *Embodiment and Virtue in Gregory of Nyssa: An Anagogical Approach.* Oxford: Oxford University Press, 2013.

Cadenhead, Raphael A. *The Body and Desire: Gregory of Nyssa's Ascetical Theology.* Berkeley: University of California Press, 2018.

Clement of Alexandria. *Christ the Educator (The Fathers of the Church, vol. 23).* Translated by Simon P. Wood and C.P. Washington, DC: CUA Press, 2010.

Dennis, Trevor. "Man Beyond Price: Gregory of Nyssa and Slavery." In *Heaven and Earth: Essex Essays in Theology and Ethics*, edited by Andrew Linzey and Peter Wexler, 129–145. Worthing: Churchman Publishing Ltd., 1986.

Derrida, Jacques. "Force of Law: The 'Mystical Foundations of Authority.'" In *Deconstruction and the Possibility of Justice*, edited by D. Cornell, M. Rosenfeld, and D. Carlson, 3–67. London: Routledge, 1992.

Douglass, Scot. *Theology of the Gap: Cappadocian Language Theory and the Trinitarian Controversy.* New York: Peter Lang, 2005.

Gonzalez, Justo L. *Faith and Wealth: A History of Early Christian Ideas on the Origin, Significance, and Use of Money.* Eugene, OR: Wipf and Stock Publishers, 2002.

Gregory of Nazianzus. *On God and Christ: The Five Theological Orations and Two Letters to Cledonius.* Translated by F. Williams and L. Wickham. New York: St Vladimir's Seminary Press, 2002.

Gregory of Nyssa. *Ascetical Works (The Fathers of the Church, vol. 58).* Translated by V.W. Callahan. Washington, DC: CUA Press, 1999.

———. *Catechetical Discourse—A Handbook for Catechists by St. Gregory of Nyssa.* Translated by Ignatius Green. New York: St Vladimirs Seminary Press, 2019.

———. *Homilies on the Song of Songs.* Translated by R.A. Norris. Atlanta: Society of Biblical Literature, 2012.

———. *The Life of Saint Macrina.* Translated by Kevin Corrigan. Eugene, OR: Wipf and Stock Publishers, 2005.

———. *The Lord's Prayer, the Beatitudes.* Translated by H.C. Graef. New York: Paulist Press, 1953.

———. "When (the Father) Will Subject All Things to (the Son), Then (the Son) Himself Will Be Subjected to Him (the Father) Who Subjects All Things to Him (the Son). A Treatise on First Corinthians 15.28." Translated by Casimir McCambley. Greek Orthodox Theological Review 28 (1983): 1–25.

Hall, S.G., ed. *International Colloquium on Gregory of Nyssa. Gregory of Nyssa, Homilies on Ecclesiastes: An English Version with Supporting Studies: Proceedings of the Seventh International Colloquium on Gregory of Nyssa.* Berlin, New York: W. de Gruyter, 1993.

Hart, David Bentley. "The Whole of Humanity: Gregory of Nyssa's Critique of Slavery in Light of His Eschatology." In *The Hidden and the Manifest: Essays in Theology and Metaphysics*, 237–53. Grand Rapids, MI: Wm. B. Eerdmans Publishing Co., 2017.

Kant, Immanuel. *Werke in zehn Bänden, vol. 9.* Edited by Wilhelm Weischedel. Darmstadt: Wiss Buchges, 1983.

Karamanolis, George. *The Philosophy of Early Christianity.* New York: Routledge, 2013.

Maspero, Giulio. *Trinity and Man: Gregory of Nyssa's Ad Ablabium.* Leiden: Brill, 2007.

Ramelli, Ilaria. *The Christian Doctrine of Apokatastasis.* Leiden: Brill, 2013.

———. *Social Justice and the Legitimacy of Slavery.* Oxford: Oxford University Press, 2016.

Schaff, P., and H. Wace, eds. *Nicene and Post-Nicene Fathers, Second Series, vol. 5.* Buffalo, NY: Christian Literature Publishing Co., 1893.

———. *Nicene and Post-Nicene Fathers, Second Series, vol. 8.* Buffalo, NY: Christian Literature Publishing Co., 1895.

Silvas, Anna. *Macrina the Younger, Philosopher of God.* Turnhout: Brepols, 2008.

Sokolowski, Robert. *The God of Faith and Reason: Foundations of Christian Theology.* Washington, DC: CUA Press, 1995.

Steenbuch, Johannes Aakjær. "A Christian Anarchist? Gregory of Nyssa's Criticism of Political Power." *Political Theology* 17, no. 6 (2016): 573–88.

———. "The Multiform Wisdom of God, Apophasis and the Church in Gregory of Nyssa's Reading of Rom 1.20 in Cant XIII." In *Gregory of Nyssa: In Canticum Canticorum: Analytical and Supporting Studies. Proceedings of the 13th International Colloquium on Gregory of Nyssa, Vigiliae Christianae, Supplements, vol. 150,* edited by G. Maspero, M. Brugarolas, and I. Vigarelli, 498–507. Leiden: Brill, 2018.

Terpstra, Martin, and Theo de Wit. "'No Spiritual Investment in the World as It Is': Jacob Taubes's Negative Political Theology." In *Flight of the Gods: Philosophical Perspectives on Negative Theology,* edited by Ilse N. Bulhof and Laurens ten Kate, 319–53. Kampen: Kok Agora, 2000.

Tinkham, Matthew L. "Neo-Subordinationism: The Alien Argumentation in the Gender Debate." *Andrews University Seminary Studies* 5, no. 2 (2017): 237–90.

van Steenwyk, Mark. *The Unkingdom of God: Embracing the Subversive Power of Repentance.* Westmont, IL: IVP Books, 2013.

Chapter 3

Love and Annihilation

Becoming Human in the Thought of St. Maximus the Confessor and Lessons from Contemporary Anarchism

E. Brown Dewhurst

The theology I am interested in discussing is grounded in that of Maximus the Confessor, a theologian of lasting importance in many Christian traditions. I especially draw attention to the way that metaphysics, cosmology, and ethics are bound together in Maximus' thought, where one can either aim toward an existence in love, which is life, or fall toward annihilation: the denial of one's own existence in love. I explore the idea that, for Maximus, human nature is something that humans are called to grow into by loving one another, the rest of creation, and through this, God. As such, acting in a loving manner is to grow into humanness and indeed to perpetuate as a person at all, since love is tied to existence. I reframe some contemporary ethical concerns in light of this urgency, where to seek to love the other is fundamental to who we are. An important tool anarchist thought can lend such a theology involves a more critical eye cast over sociopolitical and economic relations, pointing out the interconnectedness of exploitation, suffering, and modern consumerism. I argue that a theology where participation in love is the purpose of humanity cannot overlook the fact that casual twenty-first-century living in wealthy countries is built upon the exploitation of others. I thus explore important considerations that a Christian theology rooted in Maximian concerns will be troubled by in a modern context, and sit these alongside a number of critical tools and practical innovations that anarchist thought might offer. The aim of this chapter is not a compatibility between these two streams of thought, but rather that resources that take seriously the integrity and worth of a human

Fig. 3.1. *All We Need Is Love (Maximus the Confessor)*, ink on paper, 2023. Artist: Davor Džalto

person might spark more imaginative approaches to Christian ethics in the twenty-first century.

The structure of this chapter first involves an overview of key aspects of Maximus' theology. I indicate the way that the cosmic scope of his thought necessarily leads one into reflections on what a human is and how one ought to act. Informing the rest of the chapter is this Maximian commitment to the idea that loving others is tied to what it means to become human. I move from an overview of Maximus' thought to ask what this love looks like that we are called to embody. I look both at the advice Maximus gave in his own works, and draw also on the Cappadocians, whose work heavily influenced Maximus. A key part of loving others requires us to reflect on how our actions and lifestyles contribute to the suffering of others. In a modern context it becomes even more important to reflect on the way that our lives are entwined in webs of interactions that are exploitative and harmful. I propose that there are critical tools that can be borrowed from anarchist thought—a way of thinking that seeks to deconstruct reliance on such relations of power and exploitation. I focus on four things in particular: critiquing the status quo, building alternate kinds of community, addressing difficulties that arise in such communities, and articulating hope. As I do so, I express why each of these facets should be of interest to those who mean to live out a Christian ethics founded in Maximus' theology.

LOVE AND ANNIHILATION

St. Maximus the Confessor (580–662 CE) was a monk, likely born in Constantinople, who, after giving up a life in the Imperial court of the Eastern Roman Empire, joined a monastery outside of Constantinople.[1] He later moved to a monastery near Carthage where he spent most of his years. He wrote prolifically, answering theological questions put to him from monastic and lay people from all over the empire. He is most famous for entering into a dispute on the topic of the wills of Christ with the emperor, who had made a theological decree convenient for his political ends, but counter to what Maximus (and later, the Church, some years after Maximus' death) believed to be true. Maximus was accused, perhaps not unduly,[2] of treason, and was maimed and exiled for his opposition, dying shortly thereafter. His works are seeing a resurgence of interest now, particularly because his theology is robust, expansive, and offers a wealth of rich, philosophical nuance grounded in a down-to-earth ascetic spirituality. Maximus is venerated as a saint in all Christian traditions that recognize canonization, and, as such, his voice is one of not insignificant weight in Christian theology. Given the wealth of his thought, his theology has the potential to provide a grounding to later theological explorations, and attention has turned recently to how Maximus' thought can help ground contemporary theological ethics, or—more broadly speaking—the question of how one ought to live.[3]

Theosis and Ascesis

The purpose of human existence, for Maximus, is *theosis*—deification and participation in God, though not in the divine essence, which remains unknowable.[4] An end is anticipated after the resurrection where the cosmos

50   *E. Brown Dewhurst*

is brought to God. Originally, this was to be the task of humans, who are natural mediators between the extremes of the universe, capable of understanding and bringing together the disparate parts of creation through love and reason. Humans were to be the means by which the cosmos partook in God.[5] However, humans prematurely sought knowledge of good and evil, and became enticed by material objects rather than the Creator of those objects, distorting their own natures in the process.[6] Previously, humans had the capacity to set their eyes on God and comprehend the spiritual while gathering together the material, bringing together the spiritual and material within themselves, and elevating all toward God and participation in God. This was lost when humans directed their attention only to the earthly and only to the elevation of themselves. Human natural capacity for the good and ability to offer a bridge between incomprehension and the divine was severed, cutting off not only humanity but also all the rest of creation from God. This mediatorial role of human nature is however renewed in Christ, who brings together divine and human natures within himself. If humans partake in the human nature that Christ has renewed, then they can move again toward their mediatorial end, ultimately anticipating deification—harmonious communion with God in the eschaton.

Partaking in the nature Christ has renewed can be understood in Maximus in terms of *logos* and *tropos*. In the fall, human nature (*physis*) fell away from God's intended will for it.[7] God's will, in this context, is an invitation to journey toward *theosis* and full participation in God. It is thus something of a hope, an intended trajectory, and how humans relates to God—a *logos*, as Maximus terms it.[8] This is something that exists at a universal level of human nature, but also for every distinct person and much more besides. Together, these *logoi* are a dynamic web of God's intention for the cosmos,[9] holding it in place but also inviting it to participation and to become truly itself.[10] The *logoi* are God's presence within the minutiae and structure of the cosmos, holding all in existence and enabling all to participate in the gift of being. Christ, *the* Logos, is present in the *logoi* of creation and draws all to him.[11] Thus, one who aligns their *tropos*, or "mode of existence," with God's intention for them (*logos*), is one who has Christ mysteriously present (or "incarnated") within them.[12] Importantly then, the fullness of human nature is something that has been lost to us, and is only recapitulated in Christ's incarnation, crucifixion, and resurrection. To live in Christ, in *the* Logos and our *logos*, is thus to journey again toward *theosis* and toward a recovery of human nature itself.[13] Far from representing some prescribed plan in the mind of God that one must conform to, the *logoi* are something more like a timeless divine knowledge of who each of us can be in the fullest versions of ourselves. Our mode of being (*tropos*) shares identity with our *logos* when we clear ourselves of the passions—those misoriented worldly attachments

Love and Annihilation 51

to distractions that rupture our right relation with God and the cosmos. In doing so we open up space within ourselves to be receptive to divine grace, and to have the virtues evoked within us. In this way, the virtues once again become present in us, and we grow toward our *logos*, which is to draw closer to Christ himself.

While the completion of this journey is something eschatological, occurring after the general resurrection and belonging to the next life, the work of realigning one's *tropos* to *logos* is something undertaken in human history. Without undertaking the journey of realigning oneself to God, humans fail to recover their nature, which exists in relation to God.[14] Thus, we fail to become human, cutting ourselves off from God who has given us our very existence. We lapse into nothingness—a final manifestation of the rejection of God who has offered us the substance of our existence.[15] Human nature, for Maximus, is something corrupted, but which has also been renewed in Christ. It is something we are invited to reparticipate in. We are invited to learn how to become human. This is not simply a recovery of lost protological[16] human nature however, as human nature is not conceived of as something static for Maximus, but as dynamic and inseparable from its relation to God.[17] It is in human nature to journey toward becoming more than human, and to receive the gift of completion by God. Receptivity of divine grace and this standing invitation is thus something that belongs to human nature itself. Part of what it means to be human is to freely choose to partake in God and to be completed in an ever-moving rest.[18] This makes the recovery of human nature at once a "natural" process, in the sense that it was the way humans were always intended to be by nature, and something beyond the capacity of just humans, since it involves natural recapitulation by Christ, and for humans to be filled with the Spirit. Divine working, however, has always been essential to creaturely maintenance, rendering a distinction here between natural and supranatural misguided. Humans are invited to become again what was lost to them, and this invitation involves receptivity to being transfigured by the divine.[19]

All this is to say that learning to love is part of a journey of reparticipation in a human nature restored in Christ. For Maximus, there isn't one sphere that is ethical and another that is metaphysical. What it means to be human is tied to refinding humanity in this life. This is a journey that will be completed in the next life, but a journey nonetheless. Without refinding love, which is existence shared in God, there will be nothing left to excavate of ourselves in the eschaton. How then does Maximus see this recovery of human nature as taking place? What is it that humans ought to be doing in order to *be* human?

LOVE AND SELF-LOVE

Having looked briefly at the cosmic dimension of Maximus' thought, let us look at how this translates into a more personal dimension, namely how humans act. This will allow us to build up a picture of what kind of ethical activity is necessary for the recovery of human nature, and lead us into a discussion of what contemporary tools we can then use to help us articulate such a vision.

"Ethics," insofar as it concerns how one ought to act, is central to what it means to be human. How do we reach toward the kind of restored humanity that Christ offers? Or in Maximian terms: what does it mean to work toward aligning one's *tropos* to one's *logos?* For Maximus, love, which is God, can be understood through the virtues. The virtues are instances of love, distinct moments and examples of love, partaking in love, fully representing it, and leading one toward it.[20] The virtues are, in a way, pedagogical—if at any moment the loving thing to do is unclear, the virtues can be understood as the loving thing to do in different circumstances.[21] The virtues Maximus talks of principally come from Paul: "compassion, with kindness, humility, meekness, and patience, bearing with one another in love and forgiving one another if one has a complaint against the other just as Christ has forgiven us" (Col. 3:12–13), with other occasional additions like love of humankind (*philanthropias*), and brotherly and sisterly love (*philadelphias*).[22] Strictly speaking, however, one cannot acquire virtues for oneself, since virtues are love, and love is God. Rather, one clears space within oneself to allow one's natural predisposition toward God to be renewed by Christ and the Spirit.[23] Like the parable of the sower (Matt. 13), one can prepare oneself to be fertile ground, in which seeds of faith and love are sown by Christ and can grow roots and flourish.[24] It is also worth mentioning though, that there is also a natural inherence of virtue within humans, since we have natural goodness and being itself from God.[25] So we can also talk about the recovery of natural virtue, though this recovery involves creating space for divine virtue to shine within us, rather than the acquiring of virtue by human activity alone. Much of Maximus' talk of virtue also focusses on the passions, which are misdirected attention away from God who is in all things, to the material objects themselves. Maximus talks about the passions at times as almost like a childish confusion,[26] mistaking the material object itself as deserving of worship rather than God, who persists in creation and can be known through creation, as for example when one practices natural contemplation (*theoria physike*). The passions are the moments where we perceive only the material dimension and not the spiritual meaning that is shot through all things around us and points us toward God. One clears space within oneself by trying to

Love and Annihilation   53

focus attention on God and God's meaning (*logoi*) within all things, and to avoid falling into the passions and vices. In the same way that the *logoi* are the relation of all things to God and the path to the realization of a creature's full existence, the passions break the relationship between creatures and God, so that we turn from God who *is*, to the purely material, which is rooted in nothingness.[27] Just as love gathers all the virtues, then, so too does it have its opposite: self-love (*philautia*).

Self-love should not be mistaken for truly loving oneself, as per Christ's directive to love one's neighbor as oneself, but rather something more like the illusion of self-love. By this I mean the kind of worldly accumulation for the self that pits oneself against the world (and indeed ultimately against oneself).[28] It is destructive not only to others but also to oneself, and is motivated by a kind of self-love, in the sense that the self is placed on an ultimate pedestal and all else is subservient to the desire to please oneself. Of course, such a practice is not really a love for oneself at all, as those who accumulate power, wealth, and material gains for themselves too often discover. Self-love is characterized as the opposite of love by Maximus,[29] because, while love aims toward God and gathers everything and everyone else up and cannot help but incline itself toward the suffering of others, self-love obliterates the relationships between persons. It believes that the gains of the self matter more than the lives of everyone else around it, and thus it attempts to cut not only itself off from God, but also all creation about it. Self-love is like a little black hole, a gravity well that attempts to suck all around it into its destructive nothingness. It takes what is good and absorbs it into its meaningless destructive nothings for fleeting feelings of power, control, and access to the temporary riches of the world, enjoyed at the expense and exploitation of others.[30]

Of course, the political implications of such a love are not new to Christian thought. The politically charged nature of loving the poor and condemning the accumulation of wealth and power was present in the words of Christ and has been returned to time and again in Christian thought.[31] What Maximus has to offer is a robust theological framework for understanding the interrelation between usually more abstract topics in theology and the lived outworking of ascetic struggle. In particular, his doctrine of the *logoi* and his understanding of nature and its associated faculties have wedded (and expanded on) the depth of Christian metaphysics and the spiritual traditions of desert monasticism, including attention to prayer, warding away the passions, and coexisting in community.

Self-Love in the Twenty-First Century

Given that human purpose and the promise of the eschaton are tied to the choices we make in this life, it becomes important to talk about how one ought to act. Maximus himself dedicated much of his writing to this, especially when it came to giving guidance to his fellow monks on the best way to be spiritually attentive and to live with fellow ascetics.[32] As twenty-first-century receivers of his thought however, we must be aware of our differences from Maximus. Most of us are not monks, and even fewer of us are able to escape the structure of society the way that a desert monastic could in the seventh century. We live in a world deeply globalized; at once both deeply interconnected and deeply alienated. The impact of our actions is much less isolated than it was in Maximus' time. To live day-to-day, one partakes in a giant web of interactions, many of which are violent and exploitative. The impact of my actions reaches much further and the question of how to love another human becomes even more urgent in the wake of the fact that, if I am inattentive, then I passively participate in the denigration of fellow humans, who are exploited in order for my lifestyle to be maintained. The convenience of ignoring how our actions harm others elsewhere in itself is a kind of destructive self-love. It is not so grand as some of the passions Maximus' lists,[33] and rather is a quieter sin of convenience. Much like the people who passed by the beaten man on the road, before the good Samaritan stopped and decided to go out of his way to notice the stranger who was suffering (Luke 10:25–37). Like those who asked Christ, "Lord, when did we see you hungry or thirsty or a stranger or needing clothes or sick or in prison, and did not help you?" to which he replied, "Truly I tell you, whatever you did not do for one of the least of these, you did not do for me" (Matt 25:44–5), so must we evaluate not just our immediate actions, but also those that cause suffering beyond just our comfort zone. Christ is in those whom we consider to be beyond the scope of our aid. He is in those that it is easier to ignore because they live in another part of town, in another part of the country, across the other side of the world—the distance beyond which we convince ourselves our love cannot reach, despite the fact that our economic activities already extend much further.

Gaining an awareness of the way that our lifestyles under capitalism and under the state are complicit in the exploitation of other humans and the environment—the cosmos we are called to gather to God—is a necessary step in removing a blindfold that stops us from seeing the harm we are complicit in.[34] In our complicity, we cut ourselves off from loving fellow humans and God, and edge further into that self-annihilation of self-love. Reflection and opposition to systems of oppression is thus not a nicety, but a necessity of Christian living. Living in love is not a pleasant hobby that one might do to

Love and Annihilation   55

pass time on earth, but, as we have seen in Maximus' thought, fundamental to becoming human. Similarly, those who would accumulate power and wealth are, as St Basil of Caesarea put it, thieves stealing what was given in common for all the earth to share.[35] Such people destroy themselves and fail to become human, sliding toward nothingness in their attachment to substances that are nothing without the *logoi* of meaning permeating them and holding them in existence. St Gregory of Nyssa talks of such people as burying themselves in ore, making it harder and harder for the spiritual gold within themselves to be extracted.[36] And as discussed earlier, such people not only destroy themselves, but inflict pain and suffering on all the world around them. They inflict their "self-love" on the world and do not care what perishes in order for them to possess the world. The relationship between anarchist thought then and a theology like that of Maximus the Confessor, is that, as Christians in the twenty-first century and especially those of us resident in wealthy states, a critical evaluation of the world we live in is important for understanding the benefits we reap at the expense of others just by merit of being born into states that have historically exerted more power in the world. Anarchism, I argue, not only offers such critical tools, but also goes some way to suggesting replacements to the harmful conditions we presently live in.

AM I MY BROTHER'S KEEPER?

One of the principal counter arguments against active Christian opposition to coercion, oppression, and exploitation in the world, is that there is only so much that a human can do: it is to tread on divine toes to assume that one can right every wrong in a world that is fallen, and that some states, coercions, and laws must simply be accepted as tragic necessity;[37] it is arrogant to assume that a fallen human can go about trying to correct all wrongs or save everyone who is hurt, and one must instead operate within one's sphere, living a devout and pious life as best as one can, storing up one's treasures for the next life.[38] But the moral question that this proposition is really answering is "How far do my moral obligations extend? To what lengths must I go?" or perhaps "Am I my brother's keeper?" (Gen 4:9). Under this reading, critical analysis of one's participation in systems of oppression and proposed measures to counter such systems, is seen as somehow going above and beyond what one ought to do—taking on the salvific role of God to try and "save" other people. But really, such an analysis exhibits a fundamental economic failure to appreciate that one is not parachuting in to save some distant other, but that one is taking accountability for the way that one's actions contribute to inequity, exploitation, and the murder of one's fellow humans around the globe by participation in global capitalism and the infrastructure of the state.

"But I have to participate in the state and capitalism, no one asked me if I wanted to participate, I was born participating," we might hear in return. Now the moral question has become "am I obliged to take a stand against privileges I was born into and to stand up to overwhelming odds that currently rule in my favor, at the expense of another?" And to answer that question we can look at the life of Maximus, who desired a quiet monastic life, but felt an obligation to tell the emperor that he was theologically wrong, ultimately at the expense of his life. Or Basil, who was a wealthy bishop but chose to give up his wealth and, in the face of a plague, set up a hospital-commune-city, and set out not only to cure and care for those who were sick, but to live alongside them with a community of monks, who learned skills and trades in order that the city could support itself and give all it had to those in need.[39] Or to Christ himself, who, despite repeated warnings and threats, continued to preach his good news, heal the sick, talk to those considered sinners, outcasts of society, foreigners, and the powerless, and to go into temples and overturn the money changing tables, only to eventually be put to death by the authority of the land.

Christ, St. Basil, and St. Maximus could all have lived much more comfortable lives had they stayed within their spheres; had they considered the problems of others to not be their problems. We might never have heard of that carpenter, bishop, or monk who lived happily in Palestine, Cappadocia, and Carthage. These examples are important because the reason Basil and Maximus are considered saints is because, in their lives, they have done something that typifies the life that Christ led—they have made steps along the road to recovering the restored human nature that is resurrected in Christ. The evidence suggests that love is not easy. It is not convenient and it is not an excuse to stay in one's lane and await an afterlife. As we have seen earlier, we are lapsing into inhumanity and nothingness as we fail to become human by partaking in divine love. St. Paul talks of being crucified with Christ (Gal. 2:20)—that it is better to die sharing God's love, than to live and not follow in that example. After all, such a life is no life at all. In fact, to live in Christ is to die to the world, if we read on in Paul's letter to the Galatians, and it is precisely this dying to the material temptations of the world that was the task of asceticism and ascetic struggle. But such a death and leaving behind the world is not to leave behind one's fellow humans. It is to die to the passions that tempt one to "self-love," and to instead only pursue love—living virtuously and loving one's neighbor. Maximus spends much time reflecting on the inner journey of the soul toward God, but to disconnect such passages from his urging of his fellow monks to love and the struggle to get on with their enemies is to fail to understand the heart of what is meant by ascetic struggle for him.[40] After all, "love alone, properly speaking, proves that the human person is in the image of the Creator."[41]

Love and Annihilation 57

In many ways, we are even further obligated than Basil and Maximus, who saw their inaction as a betrayal of their belief,[42] since our inaction in this contemporary interconnected world does much more active harm than it would have in the ancient world. We are never just minding our own business, only moving in a blinkered fashion that fails to see the true extent of our actions: our political actions where we are complicit in allowing a ruler or ruling party to determine who is permitted to exist in society; our economic actions where we sell our labor and buy commodities in a cycle that makes profits for those at the top and keeps others elsewhere in perpetual starvation; and even our social actions, where we can walk past those suffering on the street, keep silent in a workplace, or about some other group victimized in the news. The scope of when one is meant to stop caring, and the "acceptance" that one is in a fallen world, lead one dangerously close to the apathy of self-destruction, and we return again to Christ's words: "Truly I tell you, whatever you did not do for one of the least of these, you did not do for me."

Maximus' theology then is useful for fleshing out a more full understanding of our metaphysical relationship with all creation and the Creator. In having this greater metaphysical grounding, we are led naturally to think about how this affects the actions we ought to take. For Maximus, as for many early Church theologians, there was no separation between ethics and the rest of theology. How one ought to live is bound up in the question of what humans are and who we might become. It would be a mistake to try and set out a systematic ethics derived from this theology, simply because the theology itself requires one not to separate the question of who I am invited to be from the question of how I ought to treat others. Maximus' great contribution is precisely in enabling us to think more holistically about how ethical questions interrelate with the stuff of existence. I obliterate myself as well as others when I ignore the suffering of fellow creatures. I cut myself off from God when I set limits to the lengths I will go to for love of another. That being said, Maximus is also someone who understands the importance of the minute and practical. He holds the larger picture in mind simultaneously with the reality that love is difficult and a practical affair as well as a gift to be striven for. I have mentioned briefly how one ought to strive for virtue, and I talk elsewhere about how such a consideration naturally leads one into more communal considerations.[43] The regulation of my own actions is a part of the construction of community, and the foundation of exhibiting the love of God toward others. What I wish to spend time on here, however, is reflecting on how an appreciation of the complex patterns of existing human relationships can help one think about what it means to try and love in the complex modern world. Given that economic and political relationships are much more complicated now than they were in ancient times; given that it can be hard to know how to love one's neighbor; to know who one's neighbor is; and that

58 E. Brown Dewhurst

it is virtually impossible to cut oneself off from deeply exploitative relationships, it becomes very important to be able to appraise the web of interactions that make up our lives, in order to know how to respond to it.

Next then, I turn to look at the way that anarchist tools of thought can serve Christian ethical thinking, both in terms of greater awareness of how our lives are entwined in a global, exploitative economy, and in terms of workable alternatives to capitalism and the structure provided by the state. Given the place of the state as a "tragic necessity" in the minds of many theologians, offering a counter to this apparent necessity is a particularly important anarchist contribution.

IMPOSSIBILITY AND NECESSITY

Anarchist thought lends itself particularly well both to providing a critical lens through which to consider human interactions, and to considering alternative ways of living and organizing that envision less oppressive lifestyles and societies. In exposing that our societies are entrenched in harmful and exploitative power-relationships, anarchists for centuries have been deconstructing myths that rely on the idea that humans will resort to chaotic murder if they are not part of stratified social orders that put them to work and punish them for wrongdoing. We are told that without someone telling us what to do, we will be lazy and cruel to one another and on this basis, the hierarchical structures of business and the state are upheld and always seen as a lesser evil.

Theologians who are interested in holding a worldview rooted in Maximian theology face two main problems with accepting this Hobbesian view of human nature. The first is that humanity was created good, and that it is possible to recover that goodness, hence, a belief that only chaos and death can come from natural human behavior is null and void. Love is learnable and creation is filled with the Spirit, bringing out virtue and divine love in creatures. And the second is that the societies we partake of and uphold are part of our interactions in creation. Community is not a prison but an expression of human activity. Settling for a society that regulates the worst of an imagined human nature is not enough. Many anarchist positions likewise come to this conclusion, though via different means, and end up arguing that while one is suffering, all are suffering. Anarchists have thus asked who these societies *really* benefit, if the acceptability of the suffering of some is seen as a necessary prerequisite. They have also sought to demonstrate that myths of human behavior as inherently selfish are unfounded, and on this basis propose organizing in such a way that assumes fellow humans are deserving of respect and compassion.

I look at four examples of anarchist thought and outline some of the ways this can contribute to a theological appraisal of contemporary living. The first is an example of anarchist critique of the status quo: the theory of spontaneous order, an anthropological study that concludes that, outside the imposition of hierarchy, humans are inclined toward self-regulation and helping one other. The second example looks briefly at anarchist propositions for structuring societies in a more federated manner—one that better facilitates self-regulation and seeks to dismantle exploitative power structures. I also in this section consider the relationship between this and property, unpacking some of the logic of possessing matter as rooted in what, by Christian understanding, is considered to be unnatural. Third, I outline some ideas in anarchist criminology. A key concern often levelled at anarchist thinking is— if one proposes to live without police and punishment, what will happen to all the wrongdoers? I look at some of the proposed answers to this question and identify some key places where the logic of anarchist criminology itself finds itself doing the kind of thinking that ought to be paramount to Christian theologians. Finally, I consider the "utopian" mindset of anarchist thought, summarized in the slogan "demand the impossible." I characterize it as not so much a belief that one *will* create a perfect society, but that not to strive to live in a better one is inhumane. I consider some similar apophatic approaches to human behavior in early Christian thought, and suggest that a return to this logic is a very useful one for thinking theologically about the kind of activity humans ought to be working toward.

CRITIQUING THE STATUS QUO:
THE THEORY OF SPONTANEOUS ORDER

Let us look first then at the way that anarchist tools offer a deconstruction of the myth that state power is a necessity. One of the most important critical tools anarchist thought permits is an outsider perspective on the growth of authoritarianism and states themselves. For example, in his recent book, *Anarchy and the Kingdom of God*, Davor Džalto charts the growth of "symphonia." Symphonia is the political ideology behind the idea that the church and governing power of the land ought to work hand-in-hand. Džalto utilizes both anarchist and theological positions to debunk the idea that symphonia has theological grounds (its theological basis is asserted by the Russian Orthodox Church). He instead demonstrates symphonia's historical roots in consolidation of power and political convenience.[44] Another example of anarchist critical tools in practice is Noam Chomsky's political works, which interrogate the more secretive documented interventions and ideological motivations behind twentieth- and twenty-first-century activities by states.[45] Chomsky

60 *E. Brown Dewhurst*

sheds light on just some of the insidious inner workings of state apparatus that occur behind the scenes and prop up state infrastructure. Also doing important work in taking apart the monolith illusion of the state's auspices was Colin Ward, an anarchist who worked in anthropology. In *Anarchy in Action*, he discredited the statist myth that without laws, rules, and punishment there would only be chaos and violence. Building on such ideas as Kropotkin's theory of mutual aid, where collective organizing is essential to human behavior and survival, Ward's anthropological studies looked at instances of removing constraints and laws and the reality of human responses in these situations, allowing him to develop the theory of spontaneous order.

In one example, Ward described how a Pioneer Health Centre gave families access to a social club in Peckham, London. The families could use various facilities there in exchange for a membership subscription and agreeing to periodic medical examinations. The biologists conducting the study believed they needed to observe humans who were free from rules, regulations, and leaders, so the only interventions into the social club were to prevent the exertion of authority. Observers stated that for the first eight months there was chaos, with undisciplined children screaming and running and breaking equipment. The only responses however were to give the children more stimuli, and "in less than a year the chaos was reduced to an order in which groups of children could daily be seen swimming, skating, riding bicycles, using the gymnasium or playing some game, occasionally reading a book in the library . . . the running and screaming were things of the past."[46] In a report on the Peckham experiment the following conclusion was drawn: "A society, therefore, if left to itself in suitable circumstances to express itself spontaneously works out its own salvation and achieves a harmony of actions which superimposed leadership cannot emulate."[47] Ward drew on examples such as these to propose the theory of spontaneous order: the idea that people will naturally order themselves in communities and do not need to be ruled or told what to do in order to live in harmony with one another. The period of violence and frustration in which children lashed out as soon as they had the opportunity to live without rules and punishment is a typical testament to the kind of bottled-up violence brewed under the imposition of law and order and criminalization of free expression. Once the injury of being silenced and the frustration of being helpless and subject to the will of others had faded and there was no longer a need to lash out in order to be heard or to exercise their own free will, the children were able to establish their own spontaneous order. This order was structured by themselves and willingly participated in, since it served their purposes to be able to enjoy what was around them and get on with one another.

A more contemporary example of Ward's observation in practice is to look at first responders in disaster relief. In the immediacy of disasters, spontaneous

Love and Annihilation 61

order and mutual aid can be observed, where rescuing people and providing the amenities needed to live—fresh, water, food shelter, medical supplies, and so on is prioritized above all else. Notably when the government (and, more recently, far right militias with tacit state support) moves in to help, if at all, it is often to protect property—to prevent looting and so forth, to introduce hierarchies that were previously not present, and to attempt to reinstate the monetary exchange of goods that was without thought suspended in the face of disruption to society and immediate disaster.

For example, we can look at the aftermath of Hurricane Harvey in August 2017 in Texas and Louisiana. Immediate response came in the form the fire department and locals, including local antifascists who provided search-and-rescue help, first aid, and established shelters. One relief worker noted, "When real disaster strikes, people put aside what they think about the world and begin to help each other directly."[48] Stores, hotels, and gas stations, however, engaged in price gouging, where bottled water, for example, was sold at $99 a crate.[49] The local government response in Texas was to issue a curfew to prevent looting,[50] while armed white supremacist militias travelled to the area to enforce antilooting measures.[51] It was announced that "The Houston Police Department is going to stop assisting in search-and-rescue missions to focus on going after criminals and keeping the good people of Houston safe."[52] In lieu of the breakdown of law and its enforcement and especially in the face of humanitarian disasters, spontaneous order breaks out of its previous captivity, and humans are able to help total strangers without regard for profit or being told to—a direct example of Kropotkin's theory of mutual aid and Ward's theory of spontaneous order. Such activities are seen as threatening by the state and private companies, which hurry to reassert government control and capitalist interest even at the cost of lives, as seen in the Houston Police Department announcement.

What this kind of anarchist theory and observation permits is an anthropologically informed observation of human behavior, hand-in-hand with an assessment of state practices and ideology. In doing so, Kropotkin and Ward went a long way to debunking one of the prevailing myths serving the state (and indeed all top-down authorities). They demonstrated that human organization is not reliant on centralized authority and that people are capable of organizing themselves without such direction. In the case of Hurricane Harvey, we even have evidence that local government was disrupting efforts of local life-saving organizing, thus also shedding light on another age-old anarchist observation: that the state is built to protect propertied and monied interests and not to protect its impoverished citizens.[53] Contrary to the position touted by apocalyptic movies and TV shows, humans in natural disasters exhibit an inclination to help one another and organize themselves freely in order to do so. This inclination, described as a natural tendency by Kropotkin, shares much with Maximus' belief in the natural goodness of human nature—a goodness that has to be obscured and tempted away with other things in order for it to fall afoul of vices associated with *self-love*. Similarly, Kropotkin, Ward, and our above examples indicate that systems are imposed upon individuals from above in order to prevent this kind of organizing and free sharing of resources.

These kinds of observations and social critiques offer a means of reevaluating the myth that imposed and enforced order are all that stands between human society and chaos. With these analytical tools in play, we are able start asking if it is acceptable to be a part of a social order founded on imposition and violence. The disaster relief example gives a window into the fringes of and breakdown of state and corporate power, displaying attachment to "getting back to normal" and protecting property over the wellbeing of humans. These kinds of commitments are also painfully observable the world over in COVID-19 pandemic responses, where the veneer of state and corporate power being at all concerned with human wellbeing over profits is being stripped away more clearly for all to see.

Critical tools then, like the theory of spontaneous order, allow us to conceive of human communal existence as something not written in stone, and with the potential to be altered into something better. The possible shapes of a loving community on earth have not been confounded by the present status quo, nor relegated to impossibility, but are rather obscured under trappings that benefit those with power and wealth, and perpetuate systems of oppression. Anarchist critical observations serve to undermine the reliance that Christian ethical theories have often been propped up on: the assumption that hierarchical society is a "necessary evil," and that, without it, a worse fate would befall human communities. By engaging with anarchist tools like those provided by Ward's anthropological studies, we are better placed to evaluate the institutions that structure our lives, and to recognize the part we play in upholding them. Ward's theory of spontaneous order lends itself to a more hopeful assessment of human community. It is an observable phenomenon, and one that should come as no surprise to proponents of Maximus' thought, where the belief that, though darkness and pain are unmaking the world around us, so too is there an inherent goodness that stems from the Creator who persists in all creation, maintaining its existence through love. Moreover, as I will discuss later, it is part of the Christian ethos not to settle with waiting for a better world to arrive, but to seek to unite heaven and earth here and now. The process of this effort is eschatological in itself and partakes of the communion of deification in the next life.

Applying critical observation of social and economic situations is an important part of reeducating ourselves and learning to love. We can gain an awareness of how institutions abuse general ignorance of their motives

Love and Annihilation   63

in order to justify and maintain systems of oppression. Instead of relying on these narratives written by those in power, a contemporary theology can use such critical tools to help recenter its ethics on its true task of learning to love.

BUILDING COMMUNITY:
FEDERATION AND PROPERTY

As well as pointing out that humans have a natural inclination to help one another and to find ways to live in peace with one another, anarchists have put into practice attempts to live out better kinds of community. Often in the shadow of adverse political conditions and multiple hostile foreign powers, many of these communities have struggled to survive. Throughout the last two hundred years, however, anarchists have been drawing on the successes and failures of these experiments to suggest some broad methods of anarchic organizing. The principal contribution of anarchist thought is its criticisms, and often very deliberately so, as propositions to replace current societal failures are the domain of those whom it concerns. Broad-sweeping one-fits-all solutions are considered naïve and presumptuous, and anarchist ideals do not claim to speak over local voices of those who know their own situation and are the agents in deciding their own future. There are some general broad ideas that can be built on, however, and some lessons that can be borne in mind in the realization of anarchist communities. Given that many seem to consider anarchist societies an improbability or an impossibility, it becomes important to draw attention to past successes and to anarchist theory. One such constructive idea is that of federated horizontal communities and the distribution of property to those in need of it.

In terms of societal structure, Kropotkin noted that the aim of a society should be an "organism so constructed as to combine all the efforts for procuring the greatest sum possible of well-being for all, while full, free scope will be left for every individual initiative."[54] He anticipated that free organization would see its own structures arise out of necessity, and envisioned something similar to medieval guild structures and to the syndicalist organizations of his own day. Local groups would freely cooperate with one another as needed, and a federated system would arise, allowing groups to coordinate on larger scales and across wider geographical regions. Decision-making would be made on a local basis, with the opportunity for consultation and coordination as needed.[55]

As already hinted at in his commitment to "well-being for all," Kropotkin advocated for the abolition of property and wages, and instead favored the giving of what was needed to those who are in need, believing that one ought to "Take what you need." This, he argued, is the principle already behind "museums, free libraries, free schools, free meals for children; parks and gardens open to all; streets paved and lighted, free to all; water supplied to every house without measure or stint."[56] The abolition of property is sometimes met with skepticism, but most concerns over this matter can be cleared up by drawing a distinction between personal and private property. The anarchist concern is largely not with sentimental personal items, and is more about getting resources to where they are needed in order for another to have well-being. The aim is tear down the storehouses of wealth: "The treasuries of injustice well deserve to be torn down. With your own hands, raze these misbegotten structures. Destroy the granaries from which no one has ever gone away satisfied. Demolish every storehouse of greed, pull down the roofs, tear away the walls, expose the moldering grain to the sunlight, lead forth from the prison the fettered wealth, vanquish the gloomy vaults of Mammon. [. . .] If you want storehouses, you have them in the stomachs of the poor."[57] While not what comes to mind as a "classical anarchist," St. Basil's sermon "I Will Tear Down My Barns" here encapsulates the principle that later anarchist thought would abide by. Rather than equitable redistribution, anarchist thought is more concerned with "to each according to their need,"[58] where the end in mind is ensuring that everyone has sufficient.

Of course, the distribution of property and food to those who are in need has many Christian advocates, beginning with Christ and the Acts of the apostles.[59] Notable other examples are the Cappadocians and Maximus the Confessor himself. We have noted Basil of Caesarea's sermon above—he also has another "To the Rich," in which he famously asked why one needs more than one cloak on one's back.[60] He also asked, "What well-dressed person has ever been granted even one additional day of life?" and "How long shall wealth be the oppression of souls, the hook of death, the lure of sin?"[61] "If you truly loved your neighbour," he wrote, "it would have occurred to you long ago to divest yourself of wealth. But now your possessions are more a part of you than the members of your own body."[62]

Similar exhortations were made by Gregory of Nazianzus, who said, "Let me not be rich while they are destitute, nor be in good health if I do not tend their wounds," and continued: "Shall we not finally come to our senses? Shall we not cast off our insensitivity—not to stay our stinginess? Shall we not take notice of human needs? Shall we not identify our own interests with the troubles of others?"[63] Or likewise, Gregory of Nyssa wrote, "The riches of virtue are to be pursued, but material wealth is rejected; for the one is gain to the soul, whereas the other is apt to deceive the senses. Therefore the Lord forbids laying up the latter, because it serves only as food for moths and attracts the wiles of burglars."[64] Finally, Maximus notes in his *Centuries on Love*, "The one who loves God surely loves his neighbour as well. Such

Love and Annihilation   65

a person cannot hold on to money but rather gives it out in God's fashion to each one who has need."[65]

While these theologians each went about giving up wealth in a different way, often hand-in-hand with the choice to live a more communal existence, contemporary consideration of how best to give to others can be more complex. The task, after all, is not just to divest oneself of wealth, but to give what is in abundance to others who are in need. The anarchist proposition for federated communal existence and redistribution of wealth to those in need, is thus something of a contemporary elaboration on ideas like Basil's Basiliad.[66] The elaboration on how to live communally and to give what is needed to those who lack has not exclusively been a monastic practice but also a way of life anticipated for the laity too.

Anarchist theory and anarchic experiments in communal and autonomous living, such as the Rebel Zapatista Autonomous Municipalities in Chiapas or the Exarchia district in Athens, can thus serve as an example to learn from and to inspire future possible modes of existence. Indeed, Christian communities such as that of the Diggers in the seventeenth century or the Catholic Workers communes in the twentieth century to the present, already resemble anarchist visions of organizing. Anarchist theory and experimentation offer practical resources for expanding on these on these autonomous communities, focusing on participatory bottom-up run organizing and fairer distribution of resources. They thus can contribute in an important way both to countering arguments that there are no alternatives to the present status quo, and to laying the foundations for further practical experimentation in how human societies less reliant on capitalism and hierarchy might be constructed.

DIFFICULTIES IN COMMUNITY: ANARCHIST CRIMINOLOGY

I first discussed how anarchist thought can give us greater awareness of the insufficiencies of our own society, both as an environment in which Christian love can be enacted, and in terms of the illusion of societal banality. Following this, I suggested some possible ways in which communal organizing in anarchist thought could benefit contemporary Christian ethics. I continue here to further articulate anarchist proposed solutions to potential problems such societies might face, while indicating why the anarchist approach ought to be of interest to Christian theologians.

If we wish to consider alternatives to current harmful modes of society seriously, there must also be a discussion of how to combat undesirable behavior that manifests in those communities. How does one "turn the other cheek"? How does one love one's neighbor if one's neighbor is acting in a manner that is violent and harmful to others? In an article on the topic, Italian anarchist Errico Malatesta (1853–1932) began first by stating that we must "eliminate all the social causes of crime, we must develop in man brotherly feelings, and mutual respect, we must, as Fourier put it, seek useful alternatives to crime."[67] He argued that the large bulk of crime is done out of lack, and that a society where everyone has the necessities of life already significantly cuts down on factors that incite one to commit crime. He advocated that one not resort to official judiciaries and police, since these set up new systems of oppression and privilege. Ward further built on this in *Anarchy and Action*, stipulating that violent crimes not originating in theft would *also* dwindle away in a genuinely permissive and noncompetitive society.[68] Both Ward and Malatesta emphasized treating the person in question as someone ill and in need of help. Recognizing and dealing with the environmental factors that caused such behavior is the only way to address crime, get to the root of the problem, and genuinely prevent future repetition.

In terms of dealing with crime once it has been committed, Malatesta advocated for leaving it to the interested groups themselves to take steps they deem necessary for self-defense.[69] Ward outlined problems with this position and was especially concerned about the risk of popular justice. That being said, Ward argued that to have freely agreed to partake in such a society and to desire to try and get along with others means that the kind of people involved on all sides will be very different from the kind of person we might expect in today's society to miscarry justice, and be fueled by popular retribution, anxiety, and guilt. Thus, he suggested that the problem of how to deal with crime in such a context really cannot be encapsulated or fully understood by those who are outside the conditions that would allow such a society to exist in the first place. In light of this, he noted that a local community calling to account one of their own might look very different to what we, in a society built toward competition, exploitation, and oppression, might expect.

It is also important to note that a significant number of anarchists writing on this topic have been incarcerated in prisons themselves and spent a lot of time with fellow prisoners. They thus write not just from a theoretical interest in the abolition of the judicial system but as those who have been oppressed by it and intimately know its workings and disastrous failings.[70] Aware that anarchist criminology must in some ways always fall short, Ferrel expresses its task rather to be calling "for an ongoing critical conversation among perspectives, for a multifaceted critique of legal injustice made all the more powerful by its openness to alternatives."[71] Each failing of anarchist criminology paves the way toward reaching a more humane way to deal with and prevent future crime. Thus its failings, Ferrel believes, are among its greatest merits.[72]

Love and Annihilation 67

While anarchist positions on transformative justice and crime in an anarchist society are varied and still ongoing,[73] the act of careful discussion about how best to genuinely help people while not advocating for systems that deal out punishment and inflict violence while inevitably systemizing oppression of minority groups in the process, is a conversation of exceptional importance to Christian thought.[74] How does one love one's enemy when they are intent on harm upon others? As I have discussed elsewhere,[75] the kinds of conversations happening in anarchist criminology are not just consonant with Christian thought, but essential to Christian living, and to seeking to love one's enemy as well as one's neighbor. From Christ's pronouncement, "Let him who is without sin among you be the first to cast a stone at her" (John 8:7) to his sermon on the mount, calling those who are merciful and peacemakers blessed, the relationship between "justice" and Christian teaching has always been about mercy, up until the moment where appeasing the authority of the land became important for later theologians. Still, the attitude toward crime and mercy persists in theologians like Isaac the Syrian and Gregory of Nyssa. Isaac argued that mercy was the opposite of justice and that it is the former that is Christian, and the latter that is anti-Christian.[76] Gregory of Nyssa, meanwhile, argued that mercy is the real peacemaker and that mercy tears down structures of society that exist to arbitrate between those who refuse to forgive one another. A truly merciful society would have no leaders, nor any need for locks on doors, he wrote.[77] Both these theologians' approaches are evocative to me of Kropotkin's exhortation of pity for the judge in court systems, who is truly made inhuman by their actions.

In becoming a judge of fellow humans, Kropotkin noted that "the judge, [is] stripped of every feeling which does honour to human nature, living like a visionary in a world of legal fictions, revelling in the infliction of imprisonment and death, without even suspecting, in the cold malignity of his madness, the abyss of degradation into which he has himself fallen before the eyes of those whom he condemns."[78] Kropotkin, who speaks of the judges who condemned him for political dissidence in various states, captures here something of the heart of how treatment of others begins to unmake the human. Can punishment undo what has been done? Can it contribute anything but a retributive "justice" that in its turn contributes only a larger sum total of misery? And contrary to the idea that a judge is impartial, Kropotkin implies that there is a very personal relationship between the condemner and the condemned. There is a degradation of what it means to be human in passing such a judgement on another. There are deeply theological resonances with such a position. How could passing such judgements be seen as virtuous and an act of love? It is for this reason that Isaac questions whether "justice" ought ever to be considered something virtuous and within the sphere of the human, and for this reason that Gregory of Nyssa too, rather upholds mercy

68   *E. Brown Dewhurst*

as a facet of love. Kropotkin's intuition that the judge is made inhuman and stripped of "feeling which does honour to human nature" draws close to a similar metaphysical expression in Maximus' thought. Kropotkin had an awareness that, in condemning the other, we have failed in some capacity, and lost something of human nature. Or in Maximus' terms, in failing to partake of divine compassion and mercy—hallmarks of a human nature restored through Christ's incarnation, crucifixion, and resurrection—we have slipped closer to annihilation and unmaking ourselves. Anarchist criminology is thus immersed in the kind of work that was begun in early Church theologies that lamented the "justice" of the land meted on Christ. It is concerned with how to build a more merciful society, and thus asking questions that ought to be at the heart of a contemporary Christian ethics.

ARTICULATING HOPE:
DEMANDING THE IMPOSSIBLE

An indication has been given of how anarchist thought in its critical and constructive capacities could be a useful resource for contemporary Christian ethics, especially one rooted in Maximian metaphysics. I wish to return to something mentioned a few times above and that is the idea that perpetual progress toward an end that remains out of reach can be valuable and a source of hope. I illustrate here why this idea is particularly important in anarchist thought, and draw parallels between it and Christian notions of *epektasis* and its descendants. I argue that returning such a premise to the heart of Christian ethics can help eradicate this mindset that the present is sufficient, or that change is to be feared lest it undo what progress has been done.

One of the most valuable aspects of anarchist thought is its chaotic presentation. It comes not in the form of plans and perfect ideal visions, but as a demand to do better. At its heart is not a plan, but a promise to keep challenging power and inequity and to seek well-being for all.[79] To this end, the ideas that are proposed for attempting this are unique to each group, time, and place that sought to express themselves anarchically and build a better community. This position was expressed eloquently by the anarchist Emma Goldman, who argued that to dictate how societies under anarchism will operate is to "fetter the future."[80] Those broader ideas sometimes shared between anarcho-communists—like nested federations of communities and the accountability of delegates who act as mouthpieces for decisions that are made by the local community—these ideas are secondary to the overarching aim of challenging the consolidation of power and violence, and seeking the well-being of all. The ideas serve the end, which is why classical anarchists like Kropotkin talked of a noncrystallized society—a society that should

Love and Annihilation

keep evolving and never be complacent, always staying vigilant in assessing the temptation to power and the stranglehold it can take even in the most well-meaning of communities.[81] Awareness of human greed and power and the acceptance that one's task is never done and that one must always strive for the impossible—à la the anarchist phrase "Demand the impossible!"— echoes the Christian ascetic task on earth—a perpetual striving toward the impossible.

In his essay *Law and Authority*, Kropotkin attributed one of the great failures of legal systems in his day to their dependence on rigid rules and laws that run counter to the reality that human existence is a thing evolving and dynamic. If one studies the characteristics of law, "instead of perpetual growth corresponding to that of the human race," one finds "its distinctive trait to be immobility, a tendency to crystallise what should be modified and developed day by day."[82] For this reason, when contemplating how an anarchist society would go about organising itself, this aspect of reflective, perpetual development is a key part of Kropotkin's proposition:

> This society will not be crystallised into certain unchangeable forms, but will continually modify its aspect, because it will be a living, continually evolving organism; no need of government will be felt, because free agreement and federation take its place in all those functions which governments consider as theirs at the present time, and because, the causes of conflict being reduced in number, those conflicts which may still arise can be submitted to arbitration.[83]

This is a particularly important point to note, since many critics of anarchism claim it to be too utopian or idealistic in its view of humanity or its visions for society. The absurdity of this claim is more readily apparent when one can observe that anarchist positions, possibly more than any other, are aware of the dangers of power and violence as tools of oppression, and exist as one of the few modes of political thought seeking not only to deconstruct its influence over society, but also to remain vigilant in seeking to keep it that way.

The awareness that in life there will perpetually be imperfection, but that the journey of striving to do better is a worthwhile pursuit, is an important feature especially of Gregory of Nyssa's thought. Gregory's reading of *epektasis*, perpetual striving or progress, envisions in typical apophatic fashion, that God as the goal of human existence will never be fully knowable, and that humans, both in ascetic endeavor in this life and in the eschaton, will never fully grasp all there is to know of God.[84] Rather than seeing this as a futility however, it is thus the journey toward the impossible that brings us perpetually closer to God, and to becoming more like God. Maximus does not share this exact mode of thought,[85] but he does see *ascesis* as a journey that can only be completed eschatologically in *theosis*. While he would not wish to speak of perpetual movement in the eschaton (since it is important that humans come to a final rest and completion), Maximus does see this rest as a paradoxical ever-moving rest,[86] in which one can come to know God but not fully know God, and know God in God's energy and activity, though not in essence which remains beyond human comprehension. There is thus in Maximus' thought a perpetual struggle of *ascesis* in this life, in which, even though perfection, completion, and true attainment of perfected human nature is eschatological, every second of struggling toward perfection on earth is not only important, but essential to who we are becoming and can become in the next life.

Since, as we discussed, this *theosis* is the purpose of humanity (and indeed involves the transfiguration of all the cosmos), the Christian mode of perpetual striving in *ascesis* toward something that in this life will always be beyond reach, shares some of those hopes that anarchist thought also finds itself exhibiting. There is an awareness of the human tendency to fall short, but also an awareness of human capacity to strive to do better, and perhaps more importantly, the *necessity* to try and do better (wherein, theologically, I mean learning to love is necessary to learning to become human, and we choose either this, or the oblivion of self-love).

Though in classical anarchist writers there is often a desire to decouple ethical normativity from any kind of metaphysics, it is within the spirit of anarchist writing to confer something of what it means to be human itself to the need to try and work toward the well-being of all. Anarchists by and large do not go around thinking of themselves as doing some great charity work by wanting to live in a less harmful fashion,[87] but can better be thought of as believing that it is a necessity of existence and coexistence that one strives to live out an anarchism.[88] This, I think, is the spirit of what Kropotkin was aiming for in his thesis on *Mutual Aid.* Though in places there are some normative and descriptive conflations in his monograph, the essence of what he was trying to argue is that mutual cooperation is part of what it means to be human.[89] If we do not aim to shape our lives around this form of organization, then we exist in somehow an inhuman and unnatural capacity. It is not that to strive for anarchist ideals is a privilege or a naivety then, but rather that to do nothing about current injustices is monstrous and to fail somehow at being human in itself. While Kropotkin had mixed results in tying this proposition to evolutionary theory (he correctly points out that human cooperation has been an essential part of human evolution, but edges into a naturalistic fallacy when he derives ethics from this feature), the proposition sits exceptionally well with the thought of Maximus the Confessor. For Maximus, we learn to become human, and we do this by striving for love. Love is God, and the virtues are simultaneous, distinct instances of love present within the cosmos. To be a human, out of whom virtues shine, is to be someone who reflects God

Love and Annihilation 71

into their life, someone who seeks and sees God in all things as the cosmic *logoi*, and who brings together the world around them in love, offering it up to God after the manner of Christ.

There is something of a shared philosophy then, in the comprehension that even though perfection is beyond reach, to not strive to love those around one in the fullest manner, is to become inhuman. Indeed, Ferrell, begins an article on anarchist criminology by talking about the necessary failures of defining anarchist ends. Like the apophatic task that aims toward a perfection that can never be reached, so "anarchism acknowledges and celebrates these failings, and doesn't bother to hide them behind cloaks of absolute certainty or competence."[90] Falling short of the impossible is understood as a given, but never a futility. It is precisely the journey toward an impossible perfection that means we are learning to become fully human.

Contained within the philosophy of anarchist thought then are sketches of hopes for futures less dictated by exploitation and violence. There are tools with which to critically evaluate the power-structures sometimes invisible around us, and debunking explorations that argue that not only is it possible to reach for a better world, but that it is inhuman not to try and do so. The attitude of striving and sometimes failing toward the good is one that can revitalize Christian ethics. It can provide Christian ethics with the critical tools and practical ideas to dig deep into what becoming human means and not to stop short when running up against the vice of convenience. The shared principal of dedicating oneself to striving for the well-being of others against insurmountable odds is thus something important to point out. It establishes that even though much anarchist thought has different metaphysical origins and commitments to Christian thought, like the early Christian attitude toward ancient Greek philosophy in its own day, it has frameworks and tools that can be invaluable for furthering Christian theology in its practical outworkings.

Anarchist thought, in its practical suggestions, its critical engagement with power structures, and its attitude toward struggling to do better, has the potential to open up a Christian ethics that has often sat complacent in the face of suffering that has become commonplace. The implicit takeaway for much contemporary Christian living is that, since it is difficult to love in a contemporary context, it is better to forget that reaching for the divine and learning to become human involves giving to those who have nothing. Placing value in constant struggle to do better *because* this is the loving thing to do, is a Christian value, though one often occluded. The hope in perpetual struggle then is perhaps something that anarchist thought can reinspire in Christian ethics, revitalizing a stagnant contemporary complacency.

CONCLUSION

Engaging and learning from anarchist thought and tools can offer Christians the opportunity to reorientate the material and mental architecture of our lives toward less exploitative means. I have outlined four ways in which anarchist thought could contribute positively to revitalizing a contemporary Christian ethics rooted in Maximian theology. I discussed how anarchist critical thought can help illuminate existing imbalances and exploitative frameworks in society, which run counter to a Christian ethic of love. I then outlined some alternative modes of human living that have been enacted in experimental anarchic societies in the last two hundred years. Many of these practices existed in ancient and medieval Christian traditions and some are preserved in monastic approaches still today. Anarchist studies and experiments can thus complement this tradition, expanding it as an option for the laity and highlighting the kinds of social problems that can arise and must be contended with. I further developed this in a study of how antisocial activity in society is being considered by anarchist criminologists, and argued that it precisely these conversations that should concern Christians who seek to love one another. In my final section on anarchist tools, I considered the importance of perpetual striving, once a central tenet of Christian ascetic theology. I argued that the anarchist attitude toward always striving to do better as a kind of natural necessity, is one that has deep theological resonances for a theology where learning to love is to become human, and abandoning others is slip into self-annihilation.

It is all too easy to ignore any but the immediate effects of one's actions, while turning a blind eye to one's participation in the substance and structure of violence and exploitation. It is all too easy to bury one's head in the sand and imagine that *ascesis* can somehow be confined to the convenient rather than to the cosmic. The reality of living in the twenty-first century, however, is that even fasting is no longer simply about what food one puts in one's mouth—it cannot be divorced from the fact that it has arrived via a supermarket, as the result of mass suffering and exploitation, from the underpaid workers who put it on a shelf, to the exploitation of the primary producers who farmed it, and the land that was overworked to yield it. We cannot delude ourselves into believing that love can be confined to the known neighbor whom one finds it easy to get on with, and not the stranger in a strange land, who lives under missile fire that the states we live in send into their homes. If one strives for love but turns a blind eye to the comprehension that the relative safety of one's life comes at the cost of the violence of the state and the exploitative practices of capitalism, then one does not strive for love at all. To live as a Christian has always meant being the problem to those in power,

Love and Annihilation 73

and the concerted effort to cover up this reality or to make life easier by staying quiet or cozying up to power is one of the great failures of the Christian tradition. As many great theologians like St. John of Damascus, St. Maximus the Confessor, and St. Gregory of Nyssa found, and indeed Christ himself, speaking of theology is to strive toward an otherworldly truth, one that will often be inconvenient to those in power and always put one at odds with those who wish to control and coerce other humans.

Christians then, have much more in common with anarchist hopes, and the concerted effort to try and live as one who seeks to become human—uplifting and loving the neighbor, the stranger, and the enemy, rather than passively committing to live out an inhuman existence built upon the subjugation of others. I have pointed out some similarities between anarchist motivations and Christian interests, but the real aim of this chapter is to point out that evaluating our place within violent systems and examining privilege should be the start of a contemporary reflection on what a Christian ought to do. Delving into Maximus' thought is important for pointing out that this is not just a part of being nice while biding one's time for an afterlife, but deeply essential to *becoming* human and knowing God through God's creation. St Macrina the Younger said that the chasm in the next life between us and God is as deep as the lack of love we had for others in the time that we lived.[91] And as Gregory wrote, we have judged ourselves already in our failure to love.[92] Eschatological immanence is thus not about abandoning the world but about seeing the urgency in loving it as fully as Christ did in the acts of the incarnation and crucifixion.

Anarchist thought reflects some of this urgency, in both its embracing of a perpetual struggle to do better, and in seeking to place the well-being of the other above complacency, and above the cruelties that amassing power and wealth inflict on society. I discussed some condemnations of power and wealth in prominent early Christian theology, and pointed to anarchist thought being in many ways a spiritual successor to this thought with a history informed by (as well as parallel to) Christian theology. This is somewhat incidental to the fact though that Christian thought has always borrowed important tools, philosophical or otherwise, from external sources. It is the premise of this chapter that a serious consideration of how to live out a theology like that of Maximus the Confessor in the modern world will require learning from contemporary thought like that of anarchism. Anarchist thought has been evolving on the basis that current structures are insufficient for human flourishing, and its anthropological, philosophical, and economic undertakings and discoveries have been in the service of trying to move beyond so-called static givens in society. To borrow anarchist author Ursula Le Guin's words, "We live in capitalism. Its power seems inescapable. So did the divine right of kings. Any human power can be resisted and changed

74   *E. Brown Dewhurst*

by human beings."[93] The societies we live in are not already written in stone, and reflecting on how we can transfigure society to be a more compassionate place is an essential outworking of any theology of love, and especially one where learning to love is essential to becoming human.

NOTES

1. A. Louth, *Maximus the Confessor* (London: Routledge, 1996), 4–7.

2. For the argument that Maximus encouraged a Byzantine general not to fight the emperor's wars as attested to in Letter 14, see the upcoming chapter: B. Neil and R.W. Strickler, "Letters of Maximus in the Collectanea of Anastasius Bibliothecarius: Opuscula 10, 12, and 20" in V. Cvetović, A. Leonas, and E. Brown Dewhurst, eds., *Studies in Saint Maximus the Confessor's Opuscula theologica et polemica* (Turnhout: Brepols, forthcoming).

3. See, for example, D. Harper, *The Analogy of Love: St Maximus the Confessor and the Foundations of Ethics* (New York: St Vladimir's Seminary Press, 2019); E. Brown Dewhurst, *Revolution in the Microcosm: Love and Virtue in the Cosmological Ethics of St Maximus the Confessor*, PhD diss. (Durham University, 2017); A. Louth, "Virtue Ethics: St Maximos the Confessor and Aquinas Compared," *Studies in Christian Ethics* 26, no. 3 (2013): 351–63; P. Blowers, "Aligning and Reorienting the Passible Self: Maximus the Confessor's Virtue Ethics," *Studies in Christian Ethics* 26, no. 3 (2013): 333–50.

4. Maximus, "Amb. 7," in N. Constas, ed. and trans., *On Difficulties in the Church Fathers: The Ambigua, vol I.* (London: Harvard University Press, 2014), 84.9–86.9.

5. Maximus, "Amb. 41," in N. Constas, ed. and trans., *On Difficulties in the Church Fathers: The Ambigua, vol II.* (London: Harvard University Press, 2014), 104.3.

6. Ibid., 108.6–110.6.

7. Maximus, "Amb. 7," 102.20; 106.23; "Amb 41," 108.6.

8. Maximus, "Amb. 7," 96.16–98.17. Maximus calls the *logoi* "portions of God" (μοῖρα θεοῦ), and later "predeterminations" (προορισμοὺς) and "divine wills" (θεῖα θελήματα) (via Ps-Dionysios) ("Amb. 7," 106.24). See further A. Louth, "St Maximos' Doctrine of the *logoi* of Creation," *Studia Patristica* 48 (2010): 77–84.

9. Maximus' analogy is to that of spokes on a wheel, which are brought together in unity in their center (Christ), while retaining unique distinction ("Amb. 7," 100.20–101.20). See also Maximus, "Epistula 2," in J. Migne, ed., *Patrologia Graeca, vol. 91* (Paris, 1865), 400B.

10. "For in their substance and formation all created things are positively defined by their own *logoi*, and by the *logoi* that exist around them and which constitute their defining limits." Maximus, "Amb. 7," 100.19, in *Difficulties, vol I*, trans. N. Constas, 101.

11. Maximus, "Amb. 7," 100.20–102.20.

12. On Christ incarnate in the *logoi*, see Blowers, "Aligning," 336 and P. Blowers, "The World in the Mirror of Holy Scripture: Maximus the Confessor's Short

Love and Annihilation   75

Hermeneutical Treatise in *Ambiguum ad Joannem 37*," in P.M. Blowers, A.R. Christman, D.G. Hunter, and R.D. Young, eds., *In Dominico Eloquio: In Lordly Eloquence: Essays on Patristic Exegesis* (Grand Rapids, MI: Wm. B. Eerdmans Publishing Co., 2002), 413.

13. Maximus, "Amb. 7," 96.17–98.17; 104.22–106.22. See also *Ep. 2* PG91 396C-D, where Maximus talks of "persuading the inclination to follow nature" so that "not having any discord with God or one another, whenever by the law of grace, through which by our inclination the law of nature is renewed, we choose what is ultimate" (*Maximus*, trans. Louth, 86–87); and *Ad Thal. 59* in "Quaestiones ad Thalassium de Scriptura sacra," J. Migne, ed., *Patrologia Graeca, vol. 90* (Paris, 1865), 605C: "Thus it was only natural that the grace of the All-Holy Spirit should visit those who had not by their own inclination deliberately fallen into deception, and, releasing them from their attachments to material things, re-establish within them their inherent natural power" (Maximus, *On Difficulties in the Sacred Scripture the Response to Thalassios*, trans. M. Constas [Washington, DC: The Catholic University of America Press, 2018], 413); also in *Ad Thal. 59* PG90 608A: "To the contrary, grace makes nature—which had been weakened by habits contrary to nature—strong enough once again to function in ways according to nature, and it leads it upward to comprehension of divine realities" (trans. Constas, *To Thalassios*, 415).

14. Or as Tollefsen puts it, "Human beings are obviously made such that their constitution admits a change beyond what this constitution may achieve *qua* itself in its creaturely mode." T. Tollefsen, "Like a Glowing Sword: St Maximus on Deification," in M. Edwards and E.E., D-Vasilescu, eds., *Visions of God and Ideas on Deification in Patristic Thought* (London: Routledge, 2016), 164.

15. For Maximus' definition of evil, see his introduction to his letters to Thalassios: Maximus, "Introduction" to *Ad Thal.* PG90 253A.

16. "Protological" here refers to human nature prior to the fall—so its uncorrupted state that it was originally made in.

17. See further on this topic: P. Blowers, *Maximus the Confessor: Jesus Christ and the Transfiguration of the World* (Oxford: Oxford University Press, 2016), 129: "nature is the theatre of the actualisation of movement"; also H.U. von Balthasar, *Kosmische Liturgie: Maximus der Bekenner* (Frieburg: Herder, 1941), 146, where nature is described as "a capacity, a plan (λόγος), a field and system of motion"; see also N. Loudovikos, *A Eucharistic Ontology: Maximus the Confessor's Eschatological Ontology of Being as Dialogical Reciprocity*, trans. E. Theokritoff (Brookline, MA: Holy Cross Orthodox Press, 2010), 10: "nature is an eschatological, dialogical becoming and not just a frozen 'given.'"

18. The completion of humanity for Maximus involves "rest" in God, but because God is never full comprehensible to humans, there is a kind of motion and growing in knowledge that persists even within this eschatological rest. See Maximus, *Ad Thal.* 59 PG90 608D; S. Mitralexis, *Ever-Moving Repose: The Notion of Time in Maximus the Confessor's Philosophy through the Perspective of a Relational Ontology.* (Berlin: Deutschen Akademischen Austauschdienstes, 2014), 149.

19. See further on this E. Brown Dewhurst, "Byzantine Theology and its Philosophical Insights for Transhumanist and Transgender Understandings of the Body," in *Eastern Christian Approaches to Philosophy* (London: Palgrave, forthcoming).

20. Maximus, "Mystagogia," in R. Cantarella, ed., *Massimo Confessore. La mistagogia ed altri scriti* (Florence: Testi Cristiani, 1931), chap. 24; *Ep. 2* PG91 405A-B. See further Brown Dewhurst, "Chapter 3: Virtue in the Cosmos of St Maximus," in *Revolution*, 93–128.

21. Maximus, "Liber Asceticus," in Cantarella, ed., *Massimo Confessore. La mistagogia ed altri scriti*, chap.7; see further E. Brown Dewhurst, "Three Practical Ways of Thinking About Virtue in Maximus the Confessor's Cosmic and Ascetic Theology," in H.A.G. Houghton, M.L. Davies, and M. Vinzent, eds., *Studia Patristica* 100 (2020): 273–80.

22. Maximus, *Ep. 2* PG91 405A; see also Maximus, *Myst. Testi Cristiani.* chap. 24; on Maximus and Pauline virtues see E. Brown Dewhurst, *Revolution*, 96–111.

23. Maximus, "Disputatio cum Pyrrho," in J. Migne, ed., *Patrologia Graeca, vol. 91* (Paris, 1865), 309C–312A: "It is not [as if] the virtues have been newly introduced from outside, for they inhere in us from creation, as hath already been said. Therefore, when deception is completely expelled, the soul immediately exhibits the splendour of its natural virtues . . . Consequently, with the removal of things that are contrary to nature only the things proper to nature are manifest. Just as when rust is removed the natural clarity and glint of iron [are manifest]" (Maximus, *Disputation with Pyrrhus*, J. Farrell, trans. [South Canaan, PA: St. Tikhon's Seminary Press, 1990], chap. 95, 33–34). On the Holy Spirit and receptivity through grace: *Ep. 2* PG91 405A; "Orationis Dominicae expositio," in J. Migne, ed., *Patrologia Graeca, vol. 90* (Paris, 1865), 877A; *Myst. Testi Cristiani* chap. 24. See further: Louth, "Virtue Ethics," 254.

24. See also the chiastic structure on learning to love through the virtues in Maximus' *Centuries on Love* (Maximus, "Centuriae de charitate," in Minge, ed., *Patrologia Graeca, vol. 90*, 962B I.2–3) and Louth on this (Louth, "Virtue Ethics," 355).

25. Maximus, "Disputatio cum Pyrrho," 309C–312A.

26. For example, "we mistook the superficial manifestation of sensible things as 'glory,' when in reality it was the source of the passions," Maximus, *Ad. Thal.* PG90 261B, trans. Constas, *To Thalassios*, 90, 1.2.22.

27. Maximus, *Ad. Thal.* PG90 253A.

28. Maximus, *Ep. 2* PG91 396D–397A.

29. Maximus, *Ep. 2* PG91 397C.

30. All the vices encompassed by self-love: Maximus, *Ep. 2* PG91 397C; material wealth as separating one from love of neighbor and God: Maximus, *De char.* PG90 965B I.23.

31. I discuss this in early Christian theology below. For examples in later Christian writing, see A. Bradstock and C. Rowland, eds., *Radical Christian Writings: A Reader* (Oxford: Blackwell Publishers Ltd., 2002).

32. The "century" format of the *Centuries on Love* and other similar chapters were intended for ascetic reflection. *The Ascetic Life* (*Liber Asceticus*) was also written for the express purpose of directing monks in their spiritual asceticism. See for example: Maximus, *De char.* PG90 1052B-D IV.18–21.

Love and Annihilation

33. Maximus, *Ep. 2* PG91 397C.

34. I explain my reasoning for focusing on the state in my doctoral thesis: Brown Dewhurst, *Revolution*, 172–214.

35. Basil of Caesarea, "Hom. 6 Destruam Horrea Mea," in J. Migne, ed., *Patralogia Graeca, vol. 31* (Paris, 1857), 276B–277A.

36. Gregory of Nyssa, "De Anima et Resurrectione," in A. Spira, ed., *Gregorii Nysseni Opera Volumen III, Pars III* (Leiden: Brill, 2014), 72.18–73.6 (PG46 100A).

37. See, for example, O'Donovan on the interim provision of the state, *The Just War Revisited* (Cambridge: Cambridge University Press, 2010), 6; or J. Milbank, *Theology and Social Theory: Beyond Secular Reason* (Oxford: Blackwell Publishing, 2006), 425.

38. This position is also implicit and sometimes explicit in more left-leaning Orthodox theology as well. See A. Papanikolaou, *The Mystical as Political: Democracy and Non-Radical Orthodoxy* (Notre Dame, IN: University of Notre Dame Press, 2012), 127–30; D. Džalto, *Anarchy and the Kingdom of God: From Eschatology to Orthodox Political Theology and Back.* (New York: Fordham University Press, 2021), 208–09.

39. On the history of the Basiliad, see C.P. Schroeder, "Introduction," in *On Social Justice: St Basil the Great* (New York: St Vladimir's Seminary Press 2009), 33–38.

40. Maximus, *De Char.* I.61; I.71; II.30; IV.18–21.

41. Maximus, *Ep. 2* PG91 396C (Louth, *Maximus*, 86).

42. Basil, "Hom. 7 In Divites,' in J. Migne, ed., *Patrologia Graeca, vol. 31* (Paris, 1857), 277C–281C; see the trial of Maximus, *The Life of our Holy Father Maximus the Confessor*, trans C. Birchall (Boston: Holy Transfiguration Monastery, 1982), 38.

43. E. Brown Dewhurst, "Learning to Love: St Maximus on the Virtues," *Public Orthodoxy:* https://publicorthodoxy.org/2019/03/26/maximus-learning-to-love (published March 26, 2019).

44. Džalto, *Anarchy*, 27–120.

45. For example, N. Chomsky, *Hegemony or Survival: America's Quest for Global Dominance* (New York: Metropolitan Books, 2003).

46. C. Ward, *Anarchy in Action* (London: Freedom Press, 1996), 33.

47. Comerford cited in Ward, *Anarchy*, 33.

48. L. Smith, "Hurricane Harvey: Antifa Are on the Ground in Texas Helping Flooding Relief Efforts," *Independent*, August 31, 2017, https://www.independent .co.uk/news/world/americas/us-politics/hurricane-harvey-antifa-texas-flooding -antifacist-storm-relief-efforts-a7921846.html (accessed July 30, 2021).

49. D. Soloman, "Hurricane Harvey Price Gouging Cases are Still Being Settled," *Texas Monthly*, December 5, 2018, https://www.texasmonthly.com/the-culture/ hurricane-harvey-price-gouging-cases-continue-to-get-settled/ (accessed July 30, 2021); G. Lanktree, "The Worst Examples of Hurricane Harvey Price Gouging," *Newsweek*, August 31, 2017, https://www.newsweek.com/worst-examples-hurricane -harvey-price-gouging-657576 (accessed July 30, 2021).

50. M. Harman, "Hurricane Harvey: 5 Reasons Looting Is Essential for Survival," *Libcom*, August 30, 2017, https://libcom.org/blog/hurricane-harvey-5-reasons-looting -essential-survival-30082017 (accessed July 30, 2021).

51. S.K. Burris, "Armed Right-Wing Militias Ripped for Bringing Guns to 'Help' Harvey Survivors in Houston," *Raw Story*, August 31, 2017, https://www.rawstory.com/2017/08/armed-right-wing-militias-ripped-for-bringing-guns-to-help-harvey-survivors-in-houston/ (accessed July 30, 2021).

52. B. Shiff, J. Jacobo, and E. Shapiro, "Houston Mayor Imposes Curfew to Prevent Potential Looting," *ABC News*, August 30, 2017, https://abcnews.go.com/US/houston-police-chief-warns-robbers-dont-houston-caught/story?id=49493765 (accessed July 30, 2021).

53. See further on this, the argument that the state is legalized inequality and theft: M. Seis, A.J. Nocella II, and J. Shantz, "Why Criminology and Criminal Justice Studies Need an Anarchist Perspective," in *Classic Writings in Anarchist Criminology: A Historical Dismantling of Punishment and Domination* (Stirling, UK: AK Press, 2020), 9.

54. P. Kropotkin, *Memoirs of a Revolutionist* (New York: Dover Publications, 1971), 398.

55. Ibid., 399; see also Brown Dewhurst, *Revolution*, 226–30.

56. P. Kropotkin, *The Conquest of Bread* (Milton Keynes: Dodo Press, 2010), 25.

57. Basil, *Hom.6 Destruam* PG31 273B, *Social Justice*, trans. Schroeder, 67–68.

58. Kropotkin, *Conquest*, 24.

59. Matt 5:1–12; Matt 19:16–24; Matt 25:34–46; Mark 12:30–31; Acts 2:42–47; James 5:1–6.

60. Basil, *Hom. 7 Divites* PG31 284A.

61. Basil, *Hom. 7 Divites* PG31 297B, *Social Justice*, trans. Schroeder, 53.

62. Basil, *Hom. 7 Divites* PG31 281B, *Social Justice*, trans. Schroeder, 43.

63. Gregory of Nazianzus, "Oratio XIV De Pauperum Amore," in J. Migne, ed., *Patrologia Graeca, vol. 35* (Paris, 1857), 881A-B; *Gregory of Nazianzus*, trans. B.E. Daley (London: Routledge, 2006), 85.

64. Gregory of Nyssa, "Orationes viii de beatitudinibus," in J. Migne, ed., *Patrologiae Graeca, vol. 44* (Paris, 1863), 1200A; *St Gregory of Nyssa: The Lord's Prayers, The Beautitudes*, trans. H.C. Graef (New York: Paulist Press, 1954), 89.

65. Maximus, *De char.* PG90 965B I.23; "The Four Hundred Chapters on Love," in *Maximus Confessor: Selected Writings*, trans. G. Berthold (London: SPCK, 1985), 37.

66. See Schroeder, *Social Justice*, 33–38.

67. E. Malatesta, "Crime and Punishment," in V. Richards, ed., *Errico Malatesta: His Life and Ideas* (London: Freedom Press, 1965 [first pub. c.1920–22]), 106.

68. Ward, *Anarchy*, 154.

69. Malatesta, *Crime and Punishment*, 107.

70. On this see, for example, P. Kropotkin, *Law and Authority: An Anarchist Essay* (London: New Temple Press, 1886). Anarchist Archives: http://dwardmac.pitzer.edu/Anarchist_Archives/kropotkin/lawauthority.html (accessed July 13, 2021).

71. J. Ferrel, "Against the Law: Anarchist Criminology," *Social Anarchism* 25 (1998): 5–15. The Anarchist Library: https://theanarchistlibrary.org/library/jeff-ferrell-against-the-law-anarchist-criminology.pdf (accessed August 2, 2021), 8. Page numbers refer to online edition.

72. Ibid., 8–9.

Love and Annihilation

73. For contemporary studies in anarchist criminology, see the collection: A.J. Nocella II, M. Seis, and J. Shantz, eds., *Contemporary Anarchist Criminology: Against Authoritarianism and Punishment.* (New York: Peter Lang, 2018).

74. For an overview on the importance of anarchist criminology, see Seis, Nocella, and Shantz, "Why Criminology," in *Classical Writings*, 9–17.

75. Brown Dewhurst, *Revolution*, 247–56.

76. Isaac the Syrian, "Homily 51," in *Ascetical Homilies of St Isaac the Syrian* (Boston: Holy Transfiguration Monastery, 2011), 379.

77. Gregory of Nyssa, *De Bea. Or. 5* PG44 1253B; *The Beatitudes*, trans. Graef, 134.

78. Kropotkin, *Law and Authority.*

79. See especially Ferrel's "Footnote on Failure" in "Against the Law," 8–9.

80. "'Why do you not say how things will be operated under Anarchism?' is a question I have had to meet thousands of times. Because I believe that Anarchism can not consistently impose an iron-clad program or method on the future. The things every new generation has to fight, and which it can least overcome, are the burdens of the past, which holds us all as in a net. Anarchism, at least as I understand it, leaves posterity free to develop its own particular systems, in harmony with its needs. Our most vivid imagination can not foresee the potentialities of a race set free from external restraints. How, then, can any one assume to map out a line of conduct for those to come? We, who pay dearly for every breath of pure, fresh air, must guard against the tendency to fetter the future. If we succeed in clearing the soil from the rubbish of the past and present, we will leave to posterity the greatest and safest heritage of all ages." E. Goldman, "Chapter 1: Anarchism: What it Really Stands For" in *Anarchism and Other Essays* (New York: Mother Earth Publishing Association, 1911 [first ed. 1910]). The Anarchist Library: https://theanarchistlibrary.org/library/emma-goldman -anarchism-and-other-essays (accessed July 14, 2021).

81. Kropotkin, *Memoirs*, 399.

82. Kropotkin, *Law and Authority.*

83. Kropotkin, *Memoirs*, 399.

84. Gregory of Nyssa, *Gregory of Nyssa, 'De vita Mosis' in Grégoire de Nysse. La vie de Moïse*, J. Danielou, ed., Sources chrétiennes 1 (Paris: Éditions du Cerf, 1968), 2.225.

85. On the differences between Gregory and Maximus on this, see P. Blowers, "Maximus the Confessor, Gregory of Nyssa, and the Concept of 'Perpetual Progress.'" *Vigiliae Christianae* 46, no. 2 (1992): 151–71.

86. Maximus, *Ad Thal. 59* PG90 608D.

87. See, for example, P. Kropotkin, *Mutual Aid: A Factor of Evolution* (Boston: Extending Horizons Books, 1902), xiii.

88. Alternatively, one can read anarchist thought in a more pessimistic manner— conceiving of anarchism as necessary because the well-being of oneself and others is the only thing worth pursuing, and the least bad way of going about life. Even without the "this is in human nature" commitment, the necessity granted by the idea that it's impossible to do ought else in the face of injustice lends itself to the same argument I make here. Anarchist ends are pursued out of an understanding that to not do so

80   *E. Brown Dewhurst*

would be monstrous, and that regardless of the results, it is the only option worth dedicating oneself to.

89. See Kropotkin, *Mutual Aid*, xii–xiii.

90. Ferrel, "Against the Law," 3.

91. See Gregory, *De Anima.* pp. 60.24–26 (PG46 84B) (Roth, *On the Soul*, 71–72).

92. Gregory, *De Anima.* p. 73.13–16 (PG46 100B) (Roth, *On the Soul*, 84).

93. U.K. Le Guin, "Speech in Acceptance of the National Book Foundation Medal for Distinguished Contribution to American Letters," 2014, https://www .ursulakleguin.com/nbf-medal (accessed July 2, 2022).

BIBLIOGRAPHY

Berthold, G. *Maximus Confessor: Selected Writings.* London: SPCK, 1985.

Blowers, P. "Aligning and Reorienting the Passible Self: Maximus the Confessor's Virtue Ethics." *Studies in Christian Ethics* 26, no. 3 (2013): 333–50.

———. "Maximus the Confessor, Gregory of Nyssa, and the Concept of 'Perpetual Progress.'" *Vigiliae Christianae* 46, no. 2 (1992): 151–71.

———. *Maximus the Confessor: Jesus Christ and the Transfiguration of the World.* Oxford: Oxford University Press, 2016.

———. "The World in the Mirror of Holy Scripture: Maximus the Confessor's Short Hermeneutical Treatise in *Ambiguum ad Joannem 37.*" In *In Dominico Eloquio: In Lordly Eloquence: Essays on Patristic Exegesis in Honor of Robert Louis Wilken*, edited by P.M Blowers, A.R. Christman, D.G. Hunter, and R.D. Young, 408–26. Grand Rapids, MI: Wm. B. Eerdmans Publishing Co., 2002.

Bradstock, A., and C. Rowland, eds., *Radical Christian Writings: A Reader.* Oxford: Blackwell Publishers Ltd., 2002.

Brown Dewhurst, E. "Revolution in the Microcosm: Love and Virtue in the Cosmological Ethics of St Maximus the Confessor." PhD diss., Durham University.

———. "Three Practical Ways of Thinking About Virtue in Maximus the Confessor's Cosmic and Ascetic Theology." In *Studia Patristica, vol. 100*, edited by H.A.G. Houghton, M.L. Davies, and M. Vinzent, 273–80. Leuven: Peeters, 2020.

Chomsky, N. *Hegemony or Survival: America's Quest for Global Dominance.* New York: Metropolitan Books, 2003.

Daley, B.E. *Gregory of Nazianzus.* London: Routledge, 2006.

Džalto, D. *Anarchy and the Kingdom of God: From Eschatology to Orthodox Political Theology and Back.* New York: Fordham University Press, 2021.

Ferrel, J. "Against the Law: Anarchist Criminology." *Social Anarchism* 25 (1998): 5–15.

Goldman, E. "Chapter 1: Anarchism: What It Really Stands For." In *Anarchism and Other Essays.* New York: Mother Earth Publishing Association, 1911.

Graef, H. C. *St Gregory of Nyssa: The Lord's Prayers, The Beautitudes.* New York: Paulist Press, 1954.

Gregory of Nyssa. "De Anima et Resurrectione." In *Gregorii Nysseni Opera Volumen III, Pars III*, edited by A. Spira. Leiden: Brill, 2014.

———. *Gregory of Nyssa, 'De vita Mosis' in Grégoire de Nysse. La vie de Moïse*. Edited by J. Danielou. Sources chrétiennes 1. Paris: Éditions du Cerf, 1968.

Harper, D. *The Analogy of Love: St Maximus the Confessor and the Foundations of Ethics*. New York: St. Vladimir's Seminary Press, 2019.

Isaac the Syrian. *Ascetical Homilies of St Isaac the Syrian*. Translated from the Greek and Syriac by the Holy Transfiguration Monastery. Revised second edition. Boston: Holy Transfiguration Monastery, 2011.

Kropotkin, P. *The Conquest of Bread*. Milton Keynes: Dodo Press, 2010.

———. *Law and Authority: An Anarchist Essay*. London: New Temple Press, 1886.

———. *Memoirs of a Revolutionist*. New York: Dover Publications, 1971.

———. *Mutual Aid: A Factor of Evolution*. Boston: Extending Horizons Books, 1902.

Loudovikos, N. *A Eucharistic Ontology: Maximus the Confessor's Eschatological Ontology of Being as Dialogical Reciprocity*. Translated by E. Theokritoff. Brookline, MA: Holy Cross Orthodox Press, 2010.

Louth, A. *Maximus the Confessor*. London: Routledge, 1996.

———. "St Maximos' Doctrine of the *logoi* of Creation." *Studia Patristica* 48 (2010): 77–84.

———. "Virtue Ethics: St Maximos the Confessor and Aquinas Compared." *Studies in Christian Ethics* 26, no. 3 (2013): 351–63.

Malatesta, E. *Errico Malatesta: His Life and Ideas*. Edited by V. Richards. London: Freedom Press, 1965.

Maximos the Confessor. *On Difficulties in the Church Fathers: The Ambigua Vol I*. Edited and translated by N. Constas. London: Harvard University Press, 2014.

Maximus. "The Four Hundred Chapters on Love." In *Maximus Confessor: Selected Writings*, translated by G. Berthold. London: SPCK, 1985.

———. *Massimo Confessore. La mistagogia ed altri scriti*. Edited by R. Cantarella. Florence: Testi Cristiani, 1931.

Milbank, J. *Theology and Social Theory: Beyond Secular Reason*. Oxford: Blackwell Publishing, 2006.

Mitralexis, S. *Ever-Moving Repose: The Notion of Time in Maximus the Confessor's Philosophy through the Perspective of a Relational Ontology*. Berlin: Deutschen Akademischen Austauschdienstes, 2014.

Nocella, A.J., II, M. Seis, and J. Shantz, eds. *Contemporary Anarchist Criminology: Against Authoritarianism and Punishment*. New York: Peter Lang, 2018.

O'Donovan, O. *The Just War Revisited*. Cambridge: Cambridge University Press, 2010.

Papanikolaou, A. *The Mystical as Political: Democracy and Non-Radical Orthodoxy*. Notre Dame, IN: University of Notre Dame Press, 2012.

St. Maximos the Confessor. *On Difficulties in the Sacred Scripture the Response to Thalassios*. Translated by M. Constas. Washington, DC: The Catholic University of America Press, 2018.

Saint Maximus the Confessor. *Disputation with Pyrrhus.* Translated by J. Farrell. South Canaan, PA: St. Tikhon's Seminary Press, 1990.

Schroeder, C.P. "Introduction." In *On Social Justice: St Basil the Great.* New York: St Vladimir's Seminary Press, 2009.

Seis, M., A.J. Nocella II, and J. Shantz. "Why Criminology and Criminal Justice Studies Need an Anarchist Perspective." In *Classic Writings in Anarchist Criminology: A Historical Dismantling of Punishment and Domination.* Stirling, UK: AK Press, 2020.

Tollefsen, T. "Like a Glowing Sword: St Maximus on Deification." In *Visions of God and Ideas on Deification in Patristic Thought*, edited by M. Edwards and E.E., D-Vasilescu, 158–69. London: Routledge, 2016.

von Balthasar, H.U. *Kosmische Liturgie: Maximus der Bekenner.* Frieburg: Herder, 1941

Ward, C. *Anarchy in Action.* London: Freedom Press, 1996.

Chapter 4

Holy Foolishness as a Form of *Anarchism*

Per-Arne Bodin

The aim of this chapter is to present a special form of Russian orthodox religious practice, foolishness in Christ, called *iurodstvo* in Russian, and set it in relation to the political movement of anarchism. Many similarities as well as many differences will be disclosed between the two, which at first glance are very disparate phenomena or concepts in Russian cultural history. They are, as I will demonstrate, important, not only in their own right but because they are also deeply intermingled in Russian cultural tradition. I will approach my research question from *iurodstvo*, and after having presented this phenomenon in the Russian context, I will turn to a discussion of the similarities between *iurodstvo* and anarchy.

DEFINITION

Holy foolishness is an extreme and very special form of Orthodox asceticism that has roots in Byzantium but developed particularly in Russia. It is, at least by definition, a voluntary state that a Christian enters before God, much like chastity, anchoritism, or other monastic vows. The holy fool dons a mask that outwardly closely resembles mental illness. The theological ground for such behavior includes passages in I Corinthians (3:18–19): "If any man among you seemeth to be wise in this world, let him become a fool, that he may be wise. For the wisdom of this world is foolishness with God" and I Corinthians (4:10) "We are fools for Christ's sake." For the apostle Paul, it was Antiquity that represented worldly wisdom, while foolishness was Christianity, which for him was the highest form of wisdom, outruling the classical philosophy.

Fig. 4.1. *A Fool for Christ (Xenia of St. Petersburg)*, ink on paper, 2023. Artist: Davor Džalto

Iurodstvo, in contrast, interprets the Biblical passages literally as an exhortation to become a fool.

As is often the case with the naming of phenomena in the history of ideas, it is the skeptics who gave holy foolishness its name. In Byzantium such fools were called "saloi," which refers, roughly translated, to persons who are "touched," and the Russian "iurodivyi" originally meant "degenerate, freak." The popular designation in Russian, however, is "God's people" or "the blessed" ("blazhennyie"), a word that derives from the Beatitudes. Already here in these epithets we can notice two entirely different views of the phenomenon. "Iurodivyi" still carries negative connotations and can refer to both a "crackpot" and a holy fool.

HOLY FOOLS IN SCHOLARSHIP, LITERATURE, AND PHILOSOPHY

There are two kinds of sources pertaining to fools in Christ. On the one hand there is a still-living popular narrative tradition in which they figure, while on the other there exists an extensive hagiographic and hymnographic literature dedicated to canonized holy fools. The scholarly literature on the subject is exceedingly rich, and I will mention just a few titles. A study by I. G. Pryzhov appeared as early as 1860[1] and two other major works appeared before the revolution, one by Ioann Kovalevskii[2] and the other by Aleksei Kuznetsov.[3] Kuznetsov discusses more or less all the features noted here. He does so from an apologetic perspective, however, defending holy foolishness in an age in which scientific explanations were gaining ascendancy over religion in Russia as well as elsewhere. Among early non-Russian scholars who have addressed the phenomenon may be mentioned Ernst Benz, whose 1938 article "Heilige Narrheit" is now regarded as a classic,[4] and the past thirty years have witnessed a real burst of interest that has resulted in studies by Lennart Rydén, Ewa Thompson, Vincent Déroche, and many others.

Holy fools have been an important motif in Russian fiction, and several scholars have examined *iurodstvo* in the works of Lev Tolstoy, Fedor Dostoevsky, and a number of other authors. The phenomenon has also attracted the attention of prominent Russian thinkers such as philosopher of religion Lev Shestov, who returns to it time and time again and uses it in his attack on European rationalism. According to him, there is a conflict in European culture between belief in reason and the realization that to a great extent the human essence transcends reason. He regards the Classical Greek and Roman world as representing this belief in reason, which is always, as he maintains, in vain and always ultimately proves to be false. Judaism and

Christianity, in contrast, rebelled against rationalism, and although the rebellion was betrayed by the Catholic Church, it returned with Martin Luther's doctrine of "Sola fide," which is also the title of one of Shestov's books. Thus, in his view holy fools are consistent with his notion of Christianity, and he compares them to the Old Testament prophets and the New Testament apostles, referring to the "enigmatic iurodstvo of prophets and apostles."[5]

A wave of new scholarly interest in the holy fool arouse in the wake of Mikhail Bakhtin's book on Rabelais and carnival.[6] Bakhtin himself uses the concept of *iurodstvo* very seldom, but later scholars regard it as belonging to the carnivalesque, low, reversed culture that is central to much of his work. In one context he contrasts ordinary saints and vitae with fools in Christ and perceives a crucial difference in the fact that the latter are individuals involved in a struggle and conflict with other people: "because iurodstvo is individual in character and is marked by an inherent element of anthropomachy."[7]

The best known work in Bakhtin's spirit is Dmitrii Likhachev and Aleksandr Panchenko's *Smekh v Drevnei Rusi* (Laughter in Ancient Rus'), which investigates the phenomenon in similar terms of reversal.[8] Sergei Ivanov's book *Holy Fools in Byzantium and Beyond* is the most ambitious on the subject up till now.[9] Whether or not the phenomenon and its significance have been exaggerated by contemporary scholars, it is quite clearly an important component in the history of Russian thought.

Above all, however, holy foolishness was regarded as an attempt to imitate Christ. To the holy fool and his pious onlookers, the attacks and blows he suffers at the hands of others reenact the attacks and blows suffered by Christ. The fool's humility is the humility of Christ. Similarity with Christ is a constant element in their vitae. Holy foolishness is based on the Christian notion that a person's ultimate confession of faith comes not through words but through action, sacrifice, suffering, and the surrender of his or her life.

Unlike ordinary monks, the fool in Christ did not don a black cowl when he made his vows but on the contrary, removed all his clothing except for perhaps a shirt and loincloth. Amid heavily clothed medieval secular and ecclesiastical society he appeared naked. An alternative employed especially by female fools was to dress in garish colors. Holy fools were almost always barefoot, even in the winter, or sometimes wore only one shoe. They did not shave or cut their hair and never bathed.

The fool's nakedness is often emphasized and has several motivations. It is regarded as signifying defenselessness corresponding to Christ's nakedness on the cross, and it involves both suffering and vulnerability not only to people but also to the forces of nature. It is also viewed as the opposite of the sinful and shameful nakedness of the world, for the fool's nakedness represents innocence and purity.[10] Unlike ordinary monks, fools in Christ did not isolate themselves but especially in the cities appeared openly,

Holy Foolishness as a Form of Anarchism

frequenting marketplaces, banquets, taverns, even brothels. The fool showed up everywhere that was off limits to ordinary monks and nuns, and attracted attention by offending others. His element was not the cloistered monastery but the crowd.

The fool's behavior is not meant to be immediately comprehensible but must be interpreted. It is often ambivalent: an act that at first seems provocative and sinful may upon closer examination reveal an entirely different didactic and sacred meaning. One typical account relates that Vasilii the Blessed, the Church on the Red square in Moscow is dedicated to him, poured out a goblet of wine that Ivan the Terrible had offered him. The gesture alluded to the goblets of wrath in Revelation and boded divine punishment for the unjust tsar. The real meaning of their actions was disclosed in their vitae.

It was not only the holy fools' appearance that caused offense and revulsion in public places, but also their behavior and their talk. They would play a peculiar one-man (or one-woman) theatre in which they both acted on stage and directed the onlookers. They spoke in parables, riddles, murky utterances, and incoherent phrases, sometimes also curses and obscenities, echoing, and children's language.[11]

Most often, however, fools were not especially talkative but communicated through silence and gestures. They were generally asocial and provocative and directed their behavior particularly against wealth, buying and selling, and stinginess by, for example, stealing goods from marketplace vendors and throwing the items on the ground.

Like their speech, however, these acts were madness only on the surface, for all such gestures had a profound hidden meaning that Christians were to try to interpret and understand.

Fools in Christ lived among others yet at the same time were solitary. They took their monastic vows directly before God and only in exceptional cases mentioned anything to another monk or priest. Nor did they usually have any contact with each other, and they played their form of theatre in almost total isolation from those around them. They were both inside and outside the human community. As Bakhtin notes in the excerpt cited above, *iurodstvo* is an individual saintly ideal that differs completely from other kinds of monastic life and practices.

One of the holy fool's most important strategies for attracting attention was to arouse revulsion through his ugliness, odor, and eating habits. They attacked the Orthodox Church's worship of beauty and focus on the aesthetic side of the service as reflected in beautiful architecture, icons, singing, vestments, and the aroma of holy oil and incense. They would often enter churches merely to disrupt the service by shouting, throwing things, and generally causing commotion. This was the same sort of antisocial behavior as out in the marketplace, a kind of sacred carnival performance in which conventional norms were turned upside down to shock—pretending to eat meat during a fast, for example, and blaspheming.

The fool's behavior was a reminder of the limitations of earthly beauty and a questioning of its intrinsic worth, and he was needed to establish a balance within the Church between the ideals of external and inner beauty. Moreover, far from attempting to cultivate a friendly and understanding image, the holy fool strove for wild, dangerous, and erratic behavior.

They are said to have enjoyed immunity from legal prosecution. There are particularly many accounts of various fools rebuking Ivan the Terrible, the epitome of evil. As Bakhtin and scholars influenced by his concept of carnival emphasize, attacks on the powers that be, secular as well as ecclesiastical, are central to the phenomenon. Thus, it is not surprising that, as Ivanov points out, *iurodstvo* did not really develop in Russia until the establishment of the autocracy.[12] The role of *iurodstvo* is to upset the balance in a hierarchical society.

To distinguish an ordinary emotionally disturbed person from a fool in Christ was in fact impossible, since the holy fool ought to behave exactly like the mentally ill, and people could never be sure whether they were dealing with one or the other, or perhaps both. As is evident from the vitae, this ambivalence is an important, even entirely necessary, component of holy foolishness. The Russian priest and philosopher of religion Pavel Florenskii goes so far as to assert that it is the very core of the phenomenon:

> If it can be determined with certainty defining a given behaviour as iurodstvo, this is a reliable indication that the phenomenon is not iurodstvo but only an imitation. On the contrary, real iurodstvo can only be conjectured because it never conforms to existing criteria. It might be insanity, or it might be a special and yet incomprehensible wisdom—that is how it is perceived by others.[13]

Thus, according to Florenskii's definition, the entire notion is ambiguous and impossible to pin down, apophatic by nature and accessible only through what it is not.

Liia Iangulova, a contemporary scholar of Kazan' University, addresses this type of holy foolishness from the perspective of modern psychiatry, basing her findings on cases of fools under treatment. In the late nineteenth century, persons were venerated as fools in Christ even though they had been committed to clinics. Thus, two codes—one Orthodox Christian and one medical—were in operation here, and they were used simultaneously to interpret a single person's behavior. Descriptions of the mentally ill that began appearing in handbooks for medical students in the mid-nineteenth century often resembled depictions of fools in Christ in vitae.[14] Peculiar clothing, for example, was used as criterion for mental illness. Iangulova and many other

Holy Foolishness as a Form of Anarchism

contemporary Russian scholars writing about *iurodstvo* are under the strong influence of Michel Foucault's *History of Madness*.[15]

Since the demise of the Soviet Union, *iurodstvo*, holy foolishness, or folly for Christ's sake, which is a central phenomenon in the Russian Orthodox Church, has assumed new cultural relevance in four areas: within the Church, among scholars of culture, in postmodern theory, and in the arts, as for example in the Ludmila Ulitskaia's play *Semero sviatykh* (Seven saints).[16]

The first holy fools date from fifth-century Byzantium. Their behavior was modeled on the Old Testament prophets, who often acted oddly and repulsively when they delivered their prophecies. John the Baptist is the New Testament figure who subsequently joined this tradition of prophets. One of the first Byzantine fools was a nun who Palladius reports pretended to be insane and possessed by evil spirits. He explains her behavior with a reference to the passage in Saint Paul mentioned earlier.[17] The tradition continued in Byzantium into the eleventh century, when it almost died out, but it was adopted in Kievan Rus'at the time of Christianization in 988 and reached its apogee between 1400 and 1650.

In the seventeenth century, Church leaders began to take a more unambiguous negative view of holy fools as a threat to their authority, for a questioning of both ecclesiastical and worldly power is a fundamental feature of *iurodstvo*. Peter the Great regarded them as quite simply mentally disturbed and finally outlawed their activities in the early eighteenth century. The ban did not, however, eradicate the phenomenon. Throughout the seventeenth and eighteenth centuries there were a great many holy fools in Russia who enjoyed strong popular support but were persecuted by the state and to some degree by the Church.

Scholars seldom mention Rasputin in this connection, yet it is against the background of the living tradition of holy foolishness that his role in Russia on the eve of the 1917 Revolution must be viewed. The tsar's family and many others took his power to alleviate tsarevich Aleksey's hemophilia, along with his offensive behavior and reckless deeds, as evidence that he was a fool in Christ. Even the sexual excesses attributed to him fit the context, for holy fools often shocked those around them by obscenely hinting at their own supposed depravity. Thus, this very special tradition helped the imposter gain such power over the royal family and the entire collapsing Russian empire. Indeed, Rasputin continues to generate veneration—certain Orthodox extremists have recently proposed that he be canonized.

To summarize, then, holy foolishness represented a force directed against all types of hierarchies, secular as well as ecclesiastical. All within a Christian tradition of piety, it sought to upset harmony, balance, and order, and attacked the worship of beauty, reason, and worldly culture in general.

IURODSTVO AND ANARCHISM

The similarities between *iurodstvo* and anarchism in the nonacceptance of and in the protest against ecclesiastical or mundane power as well as in the maximalism of their expression are quite obvious, as their protest against wealth and luxury and the wish to defend the poor in society. *Iurodstvo* is strictly individualistic while anarchy is collective in its essence; this represents an important difference between the two phenomena.

The behavior and actions of both *iurodivye* and anarchists are strictly directed against authorities, be it the emperor, be it Soviet rule, be it church hierarchies or dogmas of all kinds. The holy fools are free from, critical to, and harassed by both powers. Anarchy is, however, ideologized and formulated in written texts in the Russian context, primarily by Bakunin and Kropotkin. *Iurodstvo* is mainly a practice and the, so to say, ideology of *iurodstvo* is formulated by their hagiographers, in icon painting and in hymnography often much later and often after long time has passed after the death of the holy fool and very often not by themselves. *Iurodstvo* is turned into something similar to an ideology or a teaching actually by scholars from the nineteenth century up to thinkers influenced by postmodernism. The material studied has changed the material and the whole phenomenon.

Iurodstvo is perhaps the most ambiguous phenomenon in Russian orthodox tradition, and it is by its nature anti-intellectual and antirational, as being pointed out by Likhachev and Panchenko as well as defined by Sergei Ivanov: "a righteous man who assumes a guise of irrationality for ascetic and educational purposes."[18]

Anarchy, especially in the version of Kropotkin, seems to be quite contrary to the child of Enlightenment, and unambiguous in its expression; but as reflected on by Paul Avrich in his classical book, *The Russian Anarchists*, the opposite seems to be the case. He dedicates a whole chapter to the anti-intellectualism of anarchism and notes: "Russian anarchists harboured a deep-seated distrust of rational systems and of the intellectuals who constructed them."[19]

Iurodstvo is as such a denial of rational thinking, of Marxism, and other forms of "scientific socialism" that are alien to anarchism. A contemporary scholar states bluntly the similarities between the ideas of Kropotkin and the fools in Christ.

At first glance a crucial difference between anarchy and *iurodstvo* would be the relation to religion. Anarchy is far from religion, even atheistic in its essence, while *iurodstvo* is positively religious and deeply anchored in Russian orthodox religious praxis. Modern scholars have, however, discovered a religious component in different branches of anarchy.

Holy Foolishness as a Form of Anarchism 91

A two-volume study on the relation between anarchy and religion has recently been published at Stockholm University, indicating this development. In the preface to the first volume, it is noted that the aim of the study is to: "offer a critical space for the discussion of the theoretical, theological, and historical overlaps between anarchism and religion, and to cast a probing light on the rich dialogue that these conflicts have created."[20] *Iurodstvo* is a good example of this overlapping, but not mentioned in the study.

Another crucial difference is undoubtedly the social background of the two phenomena: anarchism is said to be an ideology for simple people, for workers, but is in fact an ideology for the upper class and created by the upper class for the workers, or for the masses, as Kropotkin expresses it. *Iurodstvo* on the contrary is a popular part of Orthodoxy often seen with contempt by Orthodox theologians, but nevertheless the holy fools were still approved of by the church canonizing them.

Anarchism has an ambiguous relation to violence and terrorism. The holy fools are not always peaceful in their behavior, but the amount of violence is of a quite different kind than the one used by the anarchists in terrorist acts. Both the anarchists and the fools consider action to be more important than theory, although the verbosity of the anarchists both in real life and in their books contrast with the silence or terseness of the fools.

Both the holy fools and anarchists were thought to be dangerous, enigmatic, and difficult to understand. They instigated fear and were fearful in some cases, and in literature they functioned as a gothic element.

One phenomenon is premodern, the other modern, or in some cases both seem to be postmodern in their utter ambiguity. The close relationship between them in the nineteenth century is manifested in the self-evaluation of the anarchists or the upper classes. Kropotkin quotes approvingly a Swiss clockmaker using in a positive sense the word "fool" about Kropotkin and anarchists in general: "'A communalist, not an anarchist, please,' he would say. 'I cannot work with such fools as you are;' and he worked with none but us, 'because you fools,' as he said, 'are still the men whom I love best. With you one can work and remain oneself'" (Kropotkin, *Memoirs*).

Kropotkin is not using the exact word of *iurodivye*, but "fools" still expresses a general understanding of anarchism as something besides and out of reach of common sense.

The Russian poet Osip Mandelstam, writing in the first decades of the twentieth century, defines the radical movement in the eighteenth century in general precisely with the word "iurodstvo":

> But what actually happened was that the intelligentsia, with Buckle and Rubinstein and led by the luminous personalities—who in their holy foolishness had completely lost the way—resolutely turned to the practice of self-burning.

92   *Per-Arne Bodin*

> Like high tar-coated torches the adherents of the People's Will Party burned for
> all the people to see, with Sofia Perovskaya and Zhelyabov, and all of them, all
> of provincial Russia and all of the students, smouldered in sympathy: not one
> single green leaf was to be left.[21]

Perovskaya and Zhelyabov were the terrorists who murdered Alexander the
Second in 1881. The same lumping together of these notions can be found
in writings of twentieth-century Russian emigrant philosopher Nikolai
Berdyaev; he claims that "anarchism is mostly a Russian creation" and
in the same context talks about *iurodstvo*.[22] Thus both Mandelstam and
Berdyaev noted the relationship between the two phenomena (Mandelstam
more broadly as the radical movement). The Ukrainian anthropologist Ivan
Pantiukhov likewise notes holiness in Christ and anarchism as special traits
in the Russian character as he wrote in a time fascinated with the theories
of national characters. The Danish literary critic Georg Brandes, in the
preface to Kropotkin's *Memoirs of a Revolutionist*, connects Kropotkin and
Tolstoy and discovers a similarity between the phenomenon of anarchism
and Tolstoy's Christianity. Thus, a new intellectual figure was created in the
description of the Russian thought, besides the superfluous man, the repentant
nobleman, and the revolutionary.

The Case of Tolstoy

Lenin calls Tolstoy a holy fool in his famous article "Tolstoy as a Mirror
of the Russian Revolution." Some of the symbolist writers in the beginning
of the twentieth century introduced the abstruse concept of "mystical anarchism," mixing the ideas of Bakunin, Tolstoy, and Nietzsche.

We find only one full-scale portrait of a fool in Christ in the literary works
of Tolstoy, in the short semiautobiographical novel *Detstvo* (Childhood)
from 1852.[23]

This depiction of an *iurodivyi* is perhaps the most thorough in Russian
literature. In the published version of the novel, two chapters are dedicated to
the description of the *iurodivyi* and his actions: one with the title "The Fool
in Christ" (chapter 5), the other "Grisha" (chapter 12), which is also the name
of the fool being depicted. Even more space was devoted to him in the early
versions of the novel.

The fool in Christ comes to visit an aristocratic family on their country
estate. This is the narrative setting of the description. The narrator of the
novel and its hero is the ten-year-old son in the family. We are given a portrait of a typical fool in Christ with all his essential traits: he is ugly, disgusting, and solitary, he behaves strangely, and no one knows for sure where he
comes from or what his origins are. He is very pious and has the ability to

prophesy, foreseeing the death of the young hero's mother. When the children secretly watch him in the evening, they no longer make fun of him, as they first wished to do, realizing that they have met a true Christian. The description of the scene ends with an apotheosis of this fool in Christ, more from the perspective of the adult writer than from the childish perspective of the young hero. Grisha impresses the narrator with his sincerity and piety, which is devoid of common sense. Yet at the same time, the children notice that he is not at all as foolish when he is alone; he is still very pious but acts more or less normal. This foolish behavior in public and normal behavior in private is one of the most important traits of the *iurodivyi* in general. As a whole, the description contains virtually all the common elements of this type of Orthodox holy man. The portrait is also highly ideologized in a way reminiscent of Tolstoy's works after his crisis at the end of the 1870s. We are told by the narrator what to think of the fool, and the readers are not allowed the possibility of making their own judgement of the fool's words and behavior.

There are two strong contrasts in this description of the fool in Christ. First, there is a polarization between the aristocratic environment, the details of the family dinner, preparation for a hunt, and the hint of young love on the one hand, and the disgusting but natural and sincere figure of Grisha on the other. It is significant that the introduction of the *iurodivyi* states that the young aristocratic boy had not known him previously.

The appearance of an *iurodivyi* at the mansion in *Childhood* is also part of nineteenth-century Russian life, or *byt* in Russian, even though *iurodstvo* is a phenomenon dating from the Middle Ages. This becomes clear from memoirs about life at Tolstoy's own estate Iasnaia Poliana, where fools in Christ occasionally appeared.

More important than the role of *iurodstvo* for the milieu is the element of irrationality and prophecy, which is emphasized in *Childhood* and which contrasts with Tolstoy's strongly rational tendency, both in his realistic poetics and in his later religious teachings. The moral maximalism and the conflict between *iurodstvo* and aristocratic life and manners are further conflicts created by the appearance of the fool in Christ in the novel, conflicts that will be of crucial importance for Tolstoy after his crisis. The fool in Christ in *Childhood* has not only the ability to prophesy what will happen to the family depicted in the novel, but also a gift for foreseeing the development of Tolstoy's views and manners as a biographical person.

Tolstoy after the 1870s develop a teaching with much in common with anarchism: especially his denial of the state and property. This is especially true for the followers of Tolstoy teaching, as has been noted by Avrich. The preoccupation with *iurodstvo* can be observed through the whole life of Tolstoy from the publication of *Childhood* in 1852 up to his death in 1910. The anarchistic part of Tolstoy's teaching concords with holy foolishness.

94 *Per-Arne Bodin*

In his famous article, "Tolstoy as the Mirror of the Russian Revolution," written in 1908 on the occasion of the eightieth birthday of the Russian author, Lenin calls Tolstoy a fool in Christ (*iurodstvuiushchii vo Khriste*), and calls his teachings the sermon of a fool in Christ (*iurodivaia propoved'*).[24] For Lenin, the epithet implied a severe criticism of religion, but he may accidently have discovered an important aspect for an understanding of Tolstoy's writings, views, and character. After the revolution, the *iurodstvo* had a new flourishing, but the fools were arrested or killed. So were the anarchists. The Russian liberal politician and historian Pavel Miliukov defined in his cultural history many of the authors of the 1920s, and most notably the writer Andrei Platonov as "anarchistic" in their world view.[25]

In the figure of Tolstoy, *iurodstvo* and anarchism are lumped together in the adherents of Tolstoy, in the scholarly studies of him, and also perhaps in his reflections of himself.

Pussy Riot and Piotr Pavlenskii

Two major phenomena in the last decades of Russian culture are directly linked to the conglomerate of *iurodstvo* and anarchy: the performances of the group Pussy Riot and Piotr Pavlenskii. The women punk group Pussy Riot are known for spectacular art performances, the most famous being a manifestation in the cathedral of the Savior in Moscow in 2012. Three of its members entered the cathedral, dressed in a colorful and provocative way, including balaclavas, went up to the iconostasis, fell on their knees, made the signs of the cross and sang a song beginning with a tradition hymn to the Virgin Mary and continuing as a punk song urging God's Mother to chase Putin out of the temple. The song was added in the video clip, which was the actual work of art. Their provocative behavior inside the church is reminiscent of the actions of the holy fools in many ways: the Christian orthodox setting, the provocative talk, appearance and the furious protest against both ecclesiastical and secular power. Furthermore, one of the members, Nadezhda Tolokonnikova, referred to themselves as holy fools at the court: "We are jesters, buffoons, holy fools—yes, but not criminals."[26] This relation is often noted by observers and analysts of the performance. The group's affinity with anarchism is also pinpointed by Tolokonnikova and by observers of their action. Tolokonnikova writes in the book *Read & Riot. A Pussy Riot Guide to Activism*:

> What we were looking for was real sincerity and simplicity, and we found them in our punk performances. Passion, candor, and naïveté are superior to hypocrisy, deceit, and feigned modesty. Take childish, anarchic freedom with you wherever life carries you. Take it with you to the streets, take it to dusty prison cells. Humor, buffoonery, and irreverence can be used to reach the truth.

Holy Foolishness as a Form of Anarchism 95

The truth is many sided, and many different people lay claim to it. Challenge your government's version of the truth, tell your own, and if you can, damn the consequences.[27]

What might be seen as a similarity as well as a difference is the humorous element in the action. Likhachev and Panchenko equate, for example, the fool's behavior with other sorts of medieval laugh culture together with jesters.

The art actions that have attracted by far the most attention in recent years in Russia are Piotr Pavlenskii's performances. He stands out as the next step after the Pussy Riot performance in the evolution of Russian art. The political content of his works has an even clearer function than the actions of Pussy Riot, PG, or Voina. In *Seam*, a 2012 performance in St. Petersburg, he stood on the square in front of the city's main church, the Kazan' Cathedral, after having sewn his lips together to protest limitations on freedom of speech. Casting Christ as a predecessor of the performance artists, he held a banner which read: "Pussy Riot's action was a reenactment of Jesus Christ's famous act." There was also a reference to Matthew 21:12–13, in which Jesus drives the money changers out of the Temple.

In his next action chronologically, *Carcass* (2013), he wrapped himself naked in barbed wire and lay down on the sidewalk in front of the Legislative Assembly of Petersburg. As Pavlenskii himself described the work, it was intended to demonstrate the persecution of political activists. Later the same year in *Fixation* he nailed his scrotum to the pavement on Red Square as a metaphor of the apathy prevalent in modern Russian society.

His last performance in Russia was executed in 2015, entitled "The Threat." Pavlenskii went in the middle of the night to the entrance of the Lubyanka Building, the headquarters of the Russian Federal Security Service. He sprinkled the front door with flammable liquid and set fire to it. He was arrested, and then a video appeared on the Internet, explaining the meaning of the action, among other things; he called the doors set on fire "the doors of hell," taking an expression from the Orthodox Easter service referring to the death and resurrection of Christ. He was detained and held for a long time in custody and then, surprisingly, was not sentenced to a long prison sentenced but to pay fines instead. After this experience he left the country.

Pavlenskii is also widely described as a holy fool, a connection he denies himself although he sometimes refers to his adherence to anarchy, and he states:

I am not a member of any party or any political organization. I strongly believe an artist shouldn't be part of an organization because they nurture a sort of collectivist sentiment and work toward dogmas. I strive for the Anarchist ideal.

96 *Per-Arne Bodin*

Anarchy is a total departure from that totalitarian point where every government is heading.[28]

Pussy Riot and Pavlenskii thus both adhere to the conglomerate of anarchism and *iurodstvo*. Their absolute denial of hierarchies and power structures make them close to anarchism, and their strong adherence to the Christian tradition in their practices in opposition to mundane and church structures make them concur with *iurodstvo*.

Both Russian anarchism and *iurodstvo* were created as a reaction to and protest against an authoritarian state, be it autocracy, Soviet rule, or Putin rule. The strong oppression creates an extreme, if perhaps often futile, opposition.

Tolstoy, Andrei Platonov, the group Pussy Riot, Piotr Pavlenskii—all four of them are defined (or defining themselves) as both holy fools and anarchists. The loose meaning of both concepts (both in a specific meaning, or as crackpots and blunderer in general, respectively) is crucial for under-standing their role in Russian history of ideas, or furthermore the external attempts to understand Russian culture and history. The juxtaposition of the two phenomena creates an interpretation or misinterpretation of the "Russian mind" or "Russian soul" not only from an external perspective but also from the Russian authors, theologians, and philosophers in their self-reflection on their own cultures. *Iurodstvo* and anarchy are two strong concepts and phe-nomena merging in Russian cultural history. Both are fairly, or perhaps very wide and loose, in their meaning. This means that the use of them in scholarly discourse, and especially undergoing a comparison, is challenging and often precarious. There are factual similarities between the two phenomena in the Russian context, and stressed by the Russian religious philosophers, having deep roots in the Romantic search of authenticity and identity that echo in Russian identity management of today. The close relation between the two has today turned into a lexicon definition of *iurodstvo*: Spiritual "nomadism" and freedom, reaching the level of anarchic individualism, contempt for form and for every measure, thirst for the absolute in everything, hatred for gener-ally accepted rules and the philistine spirit, are given a holistic expression in holy foolishness.

There are thus both similarities and differences between anarchism and *iurodstvo* seen in the Russian context. Both are used both inside Russia and outside, both internally and externally, to describe and analyze Russian cul-ture. The linking of the terms is forming a conglomerate of concepts that are extremely cultural productive in the Russian context, forming an imagined Russians eclectic culture in the beginning of the twentieth century, and cer-tainly also of Russian culture in general, or in the end providing an insight for understanding Russian intellectual thinking in its entirety. There seems to be a reciprocal use of the conglomerate *iurodstvo* and anarchism in Russia;

if using the one notion the other is also close. This gives it a special weight in Russian cultural history—and Russian thinking—and in the scholarly description of it.

NOTES

1. I.G. Pryzjov, *Skazanie o konchine i pogrebenii moskovskich jurodivych* (Moskva: M. Smirnovoi, 1862).

2. Ioann Kovalevskii, *Iurodstvo o Khriste i Khrista radi iurodivye vostochnoi russkoi tserkvi: istoricheskii ocherk i zhitiia sikh podvizhnikov blagochestiia* (Moskva, 1902).

3. Aleksii Kuznecov, *Iurodstvo i stolpnichestvo* (Sankt-Peterburg: Izdanie Stupina, 1913), (reprinted in 2000).

4. E. Benz, "Heilige Narrheit," in *Kyrios* 3 (1938): 33–55.

5. Lev Shestov, *Umozrenie i apokalipsis* (Paris: YMCA Press, 1964), 91.

6. Mikhail Bakhtin, *Rabelais and his World* (Cambridge, MA: MIT Press, 1968).

7. Mikhail Bakhtin, "Author and Hero in Aesthetic Activity," in Michael Holquist and Vadim Liapunov, eds., *Art and Answerability: Early Philosophical Essays*, trans. Vadim Liapunov (Austin: University of Texas Press, 1990), 185.

8. D.S. Likhachev, N.V. Ponyrko, and A.M. Panchenko, *Smekh v drevnei Rusi* (Leningrad: Nauka, 1984).

9. Sergei A. Ivanov, *Holy Fools in Byzantium and Beyond*, trans. Simon Franklin (Oxford: Oxford University Press, 2008).

10. Likhachev, *Smekh*, 81–109.

11. Ibid., 94–99.

12. Ivanov, *Holy Fools*, 285–86.

13. P.A. Florenskii, *Sochineniia v chetyrekh tomakh, vol. 2* (Moskva: Mysl,' 1996), 612.

14. L. Iangulova, "Iurodivye i umalishennye: genealogiia inkartseratsii v Rossii," in O. Harhordin, ed., *Michel Foucault v Rossii* (Sankt Peterburg: Evropeiskii universitet v Sankt Peterburge, 2001), 196–315.

15. Michel Foucault, *History of Madness* (London: Routledge, 2006).

16. See Liudmila Ulitskaia, "Semero svjatykh iz derevni Briucho," in *Biblioteka Al'debaran*, http://lib.aldebaran.ru/author/ulickaya_lyudmila/ulickaya_lyudmila_semero_svyatyh_iz_derevni_bryuho/ulickaya_lyudmila_semero_svyatyh_iz_derevni_bryuho__1.html.

17. See Palladius, "The Nun Who Feigned Madness," in *The Lausiac History*, 119–21, *The Tertullian Project: Early Church Fathers*, http://www.tertullian.net/fathers/palladius_lausiac_02_text.htm#C34.

18. Ivanov, *Holy Fools*, 7.

19. Paul Avrich, *The Russian Anarchists* (Princeton, NJ: Princeton University Press, 1967), 91.

20. A. Cristoyannopoulos and M. Adams, eds., *Essays in Anarchism and Religion* (Stockholm: Stockholm University Press, 2017), 2.

98 *Per-Arne Bodin*

21. Osip Mandel'shtam and Clarence Brown, *The Noise of Time and Other Prose Pieces* (London: Quartet, 1988), 80–81.

22. Nikolai Berdyaev, *The Russian Idea* (Hudson, NY: Lindisfarne Press, 1992).

23. Leo Tolstoy, *Childhood, Boyhood, Youth* (Baltimore: Penguin Books, 1964).

24. V.I. Lenin, "Leo Tolstoy as the Mirror of the Russian Revolution," in *Lenin: Collected Works, vol. 15* (Moscow: Progress Publishers, 1973), 202–9.

25. P.N. Miliukov, *Ocherki po istorii russkoi kul'tury: v 3-kh tomakh* (Moskva: Izdatel'skaia gruppa "Progress," 1993, t. 2), p. 408.

26. "Uchastnitsa Pussy Riot zaiavliaet o fal'sifikatsii dokazatel'stv," RIA Novosti, https://ria.ru/20120807/718523084.html.

27. N. Tolokonnikova, *Read & Riot: A Pussy Riot Guide to Activism* (San Francisco: Harper One, 2018).

28. Quoted in Banu Bargu, "The Corporeal Avant-garde: Petr Pavlensky," in Sandra Noeth (eds.), *Bodies of Evidence: Ethics, Aesthetics, and Politics of Movement* (Ges.m.b.H., Vienna: Passagen Verlag, 2018), 118.

BIBLIOGRAPHY

Avrich, Paul. *The Russian Anarchists*. Princeton, NJ: Princeton University Press, 1967.

Bakhtin, Mikhail. "Author and Hero in Aesthetic Activity." In *Art and Answerability: Early Philosophical Essays*, edited by Michael Holquist and Vadim Liapunov, translated by Vadim Liapunov, 4–256. Austin: University of Texas Press, 1990.

———. *Rabelais and His World*. Cambridge, MA: MIT Press, 1968.

Banu, Bargu. "The Corporeal Avant-garde: Petr Pavlensky." Sandra Noeth (eds.), *Bodies of Evidence: Ethics, Aesthetics, and Politics of Movement*. Ges.m.b.H., Vienna: Passagen Verlag, 2018, 101–21.

Benz, E. "Heilige Narrheit." *Kyrios* 3 (1938): 33–55.

Berdyaev, Nikolai. *The Russian Idea*. Hudson, NY: Lindisfarne Press, 1992.

Cristoyannopoulos, Alexandre, and Matthew S. Adams, eds. *Essays in Anarchism and Religion: Volume 1*. Stockholm: Stockholm University Press, 2017.

Florenskii, P.A. *Sochineniia v chetyrekh tomakh, vol. 2*. Moskva: Mysl', 1996.

Foucault, Michel. *History of Madness*. London: Routledge, 2006.

Iangulova, L. "Iurodivye i umalishennye: genealogiia inkartseratsii v Rossii." In *Michel Foucault v Rossii*, edited by O. Harhordin, 196–315. Sankt Peterburg: Evropeiskii universitet v Sankt Peterburge, 2001.

Ivanov, Sergei A. *Holy Fools in Byzantium and Beyond*. Translated by Simon Franklin. Oxford: Oxford University Press, 2008.

Kovalevskii, Ioann. *Iurodstvo o Khriste i Khrista radi iurodivye vostochnoi russkoi tserkvi: istoricheskii ocherk i zhitiia sikh podvizhnikov blagochestiia*. Moskva, 1902.

Kropotkin, Peter. *Memoirs of a Revolutionist*. New York: Dover Publications, 1971 [1899].

Kuznetsov, Aleksii. *Iurodstvo i stolpnichestvo*. Sankt-Peterburg: Izdanie Stupina, 1913. Reprint, 2000.

Lenin, Vladimir. "Leo Tolstoy as the Mirror of the Russian Revolution." In *Lenin: Collected Works, vol. 15*. Moscow: Progress Publishers, 1973.

Likhachev, D.S., N.V. Ponyrko, and A.M. Panchenko. *Smekh v drevnei Rusi*. Leningrad: Nauka, 1984.

Mandel'shtam, Osip, and Clarence Brown. *The Noise of Time and Other Prose Pieces*. London: Quartet. 1988.

Miliukov, P.N. *Ocherki po istorii russkoi kul'tury: v 3-kh tomakh*. t. 2, Moskva: Izdatel'skaia gruppa "Progress," 1993.

Pantiukhov, I.I. *Znachenie antropologicheskikh tipov v russkoi istorii*. Kiev: Prosveshchenie, 1909, https://bvs1.club/antrop/pantyuhov-znachenie-antropologicheskih-tipov-v-russkoy-istorii.html, 4.1.2024.

Pryzjov, I.G., *Skazanie o konchine i pogrebenii moskovskich iurodivykh*. Moskva: M. Smirnovoi, 1862.

Shestov, Lev. *Umozrenie i apokalipsis*. Paris: YMCA Press, 1964.

Tolokonnikova, Nadya. *Read & Riot: A Pussy Riot Guide to Activism*. San Francisco: Harper One, 2018.

Tolstoy, Leo. *Childhood, Boyhood, Youth*. Baltimore: Penguin Books, 1964.

Chapter 5

Anarchism and Orthodoxy in Latin America

Graham McGeoch

INTRODUCTION

The story of anarchism and Orthodox Christianity in Latin America is of a minority presence. Anarchism, understood as a nineteenth-century political movement linked to the thought and practice of Pierre Joseph Proudhon, Michael Bakunin, Peter Kropotkin, and Enrique Malatesta, is "squeezed" on two fronts by narratives and scholarship focusing on nationalism and Marxism in the region.[1] First, literature on Latin America focuses mostly on nationalism and nation(state)-building in newly independent Latin American states. Therefore, anarchism as a largely antinationalist and antistatist political movement is often overlooked in scholarship on Latin America's political struggles.[2] Second, labor and revolutionary literature (so-called "leftist" scholarship) is dominated by Marxist scholarship in the Latin American region. The scholarship tends to downplay or omit anarchist contributions because they were viewed as unorthodox contributions to the more prominent political project of implementing an orthodox socialism (in terms of that being set out by Lenin and the incoming Russian Revolution). This Marxist revisionism has downplayed the presence and contribution of anarchism to politics, especially left-wing politics, in the region.

Orthodox Christianity is also a nineteenth-century movement in Latin America, linked to the waves of migration in the late nineteenth and early twentieth centuries. Furthermore, just as anarchism is a minority tradition in the political science literature about Latin America, Orthodox Christianity is a minority interest in the historical and theological literature about the region. While the first Orthodox church is consecrated as early as 1901 in the River

Fig. 5.1. *An Experiment in Eschatological Metaphysics*, ink on paper, 2023. Artist: Davor Džalto

Anarchism and Orthodoxy in Latin America 103

Plate region (in Buenos Aires, Argentina), Orthodox Christians migrate to Latin America throughout the nineteenth century from the fallout of geo-politics in the Ottoman Empire, Tsarist Russia, and the Greek peninsula. The Orthodox diaspora in Latin America includes migration from the Middle East, Russia, and Greece. Often, Christians from the Middle East are indistinguish-able in the literature from Arabs and Turks (terms used to describe migration from Syria and Lebanon). Scholarship focused on Roman Catholicism in the region, or on the entry and rise of Protestantism from the nineteenth century onward, overlooks the Orthodox presence in Latin America.

Anarchism, and anarchist ideas, enter Latin America as early as the 1860s. The French Antilles has groups affiliated to the First International, and soon Mexico, the River Plate region (Argentina and Uruguay), followed by Chile, Peru, Ecuador, Panama, and Guatemala have peasant movements, student libertarians, and working-class struggles informed by the ideas and practices of Proudhon and Bakunin.[3] Not all Latin American countries developed formally organized (or affiliated) anarchist labor movements, but anarchist ideas circulated fairly freely amongst a number of different kinds of groups, ranging from trade unions to the military. Anarchism spread through organiz-ing, class struggle, and particularly through the arts (literature, theatre, and pamphlets). Angel J. Cappelletti notes leading artistic figures from the region flirted with or committed to anarchism, including the Argentinian writer Jorge Luis Borges and the Brazilian musician Carlos Gomes.[4] There were also a number of practical and educational communitarian initiatives, which drew anarchists into close contact with indigenous peoples in Argentina, Mexico, and Peru.

Angel J. Cappelletti stresses the importance of understanding anarchism in Latin America as a European import to Latin America, and one that circulated amongst the different groups (national, ethnic, and linguistic) identified by the waves of migration to Latin America in the nineteenth and early twentieth centuries. In particular, Latin America's relationship with anarchism is shaped profoundly by anarcho-syndicalism (a revolutionary antipolitical movement), which in turn is influenced by the waves of Italian, German, Slavic, and Spanish migration to Latin America at the turn of the twentieth century.[5]

This observation is noteworthy for two reasons. First, following the Bolshevik Revolution (1917), anarcho-syndicalism morphed into anarcho-bolshevism,[6] between 1918 and 1923, with anarchists in Argentina, Uruguay, Brazil, and Mexico supporting Lenin and the Soviet government.[7] Second, the links between anarchism and foreignness helped to squeeze anarchism in Latin America during the fascist coups of the 1930s across the region and with the rise of a nationalist-populism linked to the armed forces. Even in the sec-ond half of the twentieth century, the ideas of *nuestra América* came to influ-ence leftist movements and scholarship, most notably, liberation theology.

104 *Graham McGeoch*

José Mariátegui's indigenous socialism influences Gustavo Gutierrez's work more than the anarchists Flora Tristan and Manuel Gonzalez Prada. Other liberation theologians have been reticent to engage anarchism, with a few notable exceptions including Juan Luis Segundo, Franz Hinkelammert, and Jung Mo Sung. This is largely due to the dispute between Marxists and Anarchists in the region with relation to revolutionary utopias. This is perhaps best exemplified by the mythical place in popular liberation theology (and amongst the scholars) of the Cuban Revolution, while the Zapatista uprising is peripheral to the development of twenty-first-century liberation theology.[8] The Zapatista agenda is more deeply rooted in libertarianism promoting a world within many worlds. It is worth noting, however, that the Zapatists take their name from Emiliano Zapata, an influential exponent of agrarian reform during the Mexican Revolution (1910), rather than his anarchist contemporaries Flores Magon and Praxedis Guerrero.

ORTHODOXY AND ANARCHISM
IN LATIN AMERICA

What emerges from the literature, despite the squeeze on anarchism as a political movement and Orthodoxy Christianity as an import on waves of migration, is the presence and contribution of both to political practice in the region. Davor Džalto has observed that that anarchism has never been a unified, organized movement or a coherent teaching. Rather, anarchism is a "tendency . . . that is critical of power structures and the exercise of power and authority, and that seeks to dismantle those structures whenever their existence cannot be justified, and to resist the illegitimate exercise of power across the whole range of social networks."[9] Džalto's observation about anarchism is found in peasant movements and urban movements of intellectuals and working class in Latin America. The anarchist tendency and movement in Latin America has a direct connection to a number of leading figures of anarchism as a political movement. Michael Bakunin, for example, spent two weeks in Panama in 1861 as part of his journey through four years of exile taking in Japan, Europe, and the Americas.[10]

However, Latin American anarchism is also indebted to an Orthodox Christian. A leading figure in promoting anarchism and libertarian socialism in Mexico is Plotino C. Rhodakanaty. He published the first anarchist pamphlets in Mexico. His *Cartilla Socialista* (1861) is considered the first anarchist pamphlet in Latin America. His stay (1861–1886) sowed the seeds of class struggle and pacifism as the basis of anarchism and social struggles in Mexico. Importantly, Rhodakanaty's texts continued to be published and distributed through Mexico and Latin America after he left the region.

The presence of Bakunin and Rhodakanaty in Latin America and their influence on Latin American anarchism is particularly interesting for reflections about anarchism and Orthodoxy in Latin America. Both anarchists, fruit of Orthodoxy in Russia and Greece, have very different views in their anarchist practices regarding Orthodoxy. Davor Džalto has noted that Bakunin's "bitterly antichurch and antireligion" is rooted in his opposition to oppressive state structures supported by ecclesial structures and the ideology of a certain kind of Orthodox Christianity.[11] The specific context for the development of Bakunin's "bitter" perspective is Tsarist Russia. His critique of religion, therefore, is rooted in an experience of Russian Orthodox Christianity and his rejection of that form Orthodox Christianity in Tsarist Russia. Rhodakanaty advocates a quite different approach within anarchism in Mexico. Like Bakunin, he shared an aristocratic background (his Greek, while Bakunin's is Russian), an interest in German idealist philosophy, a commitment to peoples' struggles to overcome imperialism, and the direct influence of Proudhon from their time spent together in Paris.[12]

However, Rhodakanaty does not share Bakunin's "bitter" rejection of Orthodoxy. Cappelletti notes that Rhodakanaty "argues for the necessity of religion and the superiority of Christianity over all other religions."[13] Rhodakanaty also presents two interesting readings of (Orthodox) Christianity, which will prove important to versions of anarchism sympathetic to Christianity, and to understandings of Orthodoxy in the twentieth century. First, Rhodakanaty is clear that both Roman Catholicism and Protestantism "degrade" primitive and authentic Christianity. In this, Rhodokanaty is anticipating Orthodox critiques of the "Western Church" in the twentieth century. These critiques are led, most influentially, by Georges Florovsky, but are present in other Orthodox theologians from Sergius Bulgakov to Christos Yananras. Rhodakanaty reads Roman Catholicism and Protestantism as assimilating too much of Enlightenment rationalism at the expense of Patristics. Rhodakanaty also roots the anarchist principles of love, freedom, and equality in a primitive form of Christianity without priesthood, dogma, liturgy, and hierarchy.[14]

Plotino C. Rhodokanaty was derided as an imposter. The Roman Catholic bishop Vallverde y Telles described him as a Mexican medic presenting as a Greek. Such disparaging remarks, religious slighting coupled with xenophobia, was not uncommon in a Latin America dominated by narratives of nationalism and Roman Catholicism. A Greek Orthodox medic fitted neither the national nor the religious mold in Mexico. The fact that Rhodokanaty's pantosofic (*panteosófica* in the Spanish texts) doctrine was central to both his anarchism and Christianity further troubled the bishop.[15]

Rhodokanaty was born in Athens, Greece in 1828. As a child, his mother (a widow) took him to live in Vienna where he went on to become a medic. He visited Budapest in 1848, during the revolution, before settling in Berlin to continue his university career. Berlin brought him into contact with socialist philosophy and intellectuals. In 1857, he moved to Paris. It was there that it appears that he first came into contact with Mexicans, and the political discussions related to Mexico. By 1860, Rhodokanaty had moved to Barcelona with the intention of setting sail for Mexico. He arrived in Veracruz, Mexico in 1861. Alongside his work as a medic and writer, Rhodokanaty gathered young people into philosophical discussions on the social problems facing Mexico. He moved to Chalco to be among the peasant communities, and formed agricultural communities and "free schools" along anarchist lines. Indeed, one of his pupils, Julio Lopez, participated in a peasant rebellion in 1868. The government, later in 1868, killed Lopez. In 1871, Rhodokanaty was one of the founders of *La Social*, a socialist and philanthropic organization in Mexico. He went on to be editor of a number of newspapers and published regularly on religion and politics. He left Mexico in 1886, dedicating himself to a "school of transcendental philosophy."[16]

In the *Cartilla Socialista* (1861), Rhodokanaty sets out to introduce and interpret Charles Fourier's ideas for a Mexican audience. Rhodokanaty dedicates the *Cartilla Socialista* to rural peasants and the urban working class. In the nineteenth century, Mexico was a largely rural society. Nationalism predominated among urban elites, making difficult the entry of foreign pamphlets and foreign ideas. José C. Valades's twentieth-century introduction to the *Cartilla Socialista* notes that Robert Owen's ideas were the first foreign socialist and anarchist ideas to penetrate Mexico's intellectual classes. Mexico was isolated from the intellectual developments in Europe. Europe was urbanizing and industrializing, while Mexico was mainly rural. Liberal elites later begun to introduce Proudhon's ideas. According to Valades, this gave anarchism, and particularly Rhodokanaty's anarchism in Mexico, the twin focus of justice and freedom.

However, Owen and Proudhons' introductions to Mexico were sporadic not systematic. Rhodokanaty's pamphlet provides perhaps the first systematic introduction to anarchism, a synthesis of Fourier for a very specific audience that had not been reached yet by the ideas of Owen and Proudhon. Rhodokanaty calls his system "Free Socialism." It has four major principles: the concept of a great human family; the transfiguration of the human family; an ending of poverty; and an extinguishing of authority. The specific principles, addressed to rural peasants and urban working classes, fit within a wider Mexican socialist/anarchist discussion that revolved around proposals to end war, religious intolerance, trade rivalries, and to overcome poverty.

Cartilla Socialista opens with Rhodokanaty's observation that Jesus preached the doctrine of socialism to twelve fishermen, and that this doctrine was lost to the Imperial ambitions of Rome.[17] It is both a political and religious critique of Western polities and the Latin Church. The text of the *Cartilla Socialista* is presented as a dialogue between someone asking questions and Rhodokanaty answering each question in turn. To the question, what is the perfect social state, Rhodokanaty replies: conceiving an order of free association of individuals, families, and peoples to produce the common good and to oppose the state.[18] Rhodokanaty goes on to interpret the political requirement of revolution as a (spiritual) search for harmony rooted in what he calls innate judicial, moral, or religious forms.[19] The outcome of this revolution is the absolute freedom of the individual.[20]

The role of Orthodoxy in the *Cartilla Socialista* appears to be that of underpinning eternal freedom. Rhodokanaty is aware of the tensions between order and freedom. The category of eternal religion allows Rhodokanaty to be critical of any freedoms that are curbed by political, social, or religious orders that restrict freedom. The journal *El Socialista*, in a biography of Rhodokanaty published in 1877, described him as a founder of a transcendental society of women and men, a defender of the working classes, promoter of moral universals, stimulator of agrarian reform and redemption of indigenous peoples. All of this was inspired by the Gospels, which he used as his moral basis and which informed his anticlericalism.[21] Indeed, in many of his public discourses, Rhodokanaty turns to God (not only the Gospels) to address the evils of European Imperialism, advance his idea of cosmopolitan humanity, and to advocate for the social emancipation of women. Christian education is a major conduit to eternal and temporal happiness, according to Rhodokanaty. However, he is careful (like many Latin American contemporaries) to distinguish between the good of Christianity and the evil of the Church, through his anticlerical stance. Rhodokanaty's anticlericalism is much more in tune with Latin American anarchism than Bakunin's antireligion.

Understanding of the role Rhodokanaty's religion (Orthodox Christianity) in promoting the anarchist tendencies of love, freedom, and equality in the Mexican struggle finds echoes in Davor Džalto's wider study about anarchism and Orthodoxy. Džalto identifies and analyses what he calls a "proto-anarchism in Orthodoxy."[22] In part, Džalto's proposal of a "proto-anarchism in Orthodoxy" depends on a rereading of Patristic sources in primitive Christianity, and in part on the association of this movement with Berdyaev's exploration of freedom, creativity, and love. In both cases, Džalto (like Rhodakanaty) implies that tendencies of freedom, love, and creativity (love, freedom, and equality in Rhodakanaty's vision) are a shared root of anarchism and Orthodox theology.

Rhodakanaty's sympathetic inclusion of primitive Christianity in the anarchist practice in Latin America finds echoes in the importance and influence of another Orthodox intellectual within Latin American anarchism: Leo Toltstoy. Tolstoy's appeal as a literary figure helped to embed his anarchism

108 *Graham McGeoch*

in different sectors across the continent. He appealed to intellectual and urban elites, particularly those with libertarian agendas. His practical and educational approach in establishing "anarchist colonies" appealed to working-class social movements looking for viable alternative models of human community free from state and church hierarchies.

José Julian Llaguno Thomas notes that Tolstoy's writing was amongst the most widely circulated in working-class pamphlets and cultural magazines in early twentieth-century Latin America.[23] Tolstoy was also, like Rhodakanaty, influential in spreading the anarchist practice of pacifism throughout the region, particularly in Costa Rica.[24] (To this day, Costa Rica is an exception in Latin America as a country without a standing military, and regarded as amongst the most egalitarian societies in the region.) The reception of Tolstoy's anarchism in Costa Rica was aided by his direct links to Proudhon, Bakunin, and Kropotkin.

His promotion of a primitive Christianity as an alternative to the unjust, immoral, and unnecessary modern state and church enabled anarchism in Latin America to tap into the deep well of Christianity across the continent while also contesting (and rejecting) the Church. The reception of Tolstoy's Christianity as a critique of state and church power structures and social hierarchies will prove to be a lasting influence on such contrasting political movements led by liberals and libertarians (to a large extent, the architects of the newly independent nation-states in Latin America) and Marxists and anarchists pushing for a social-political revolution in the region.

The influence of Bakunin, Rhodakanaty, and Tolstoy on anarchism as a political movement in Latin America is remarkable, particularly in light of the fact that all proceed from the milieu of Orthodox Christianity and either their bitter rejection of Christianity or a promotion of a primitive form Christianity as critical theory is directly related to their experience of Orthodoxy. It would be wrong to leave the impression that Rhodakanaty and Tolstoys' Christianity as critical theory exercised and exercises more influence in the region than Bakunin's anticlerical and antireligious anarchism. However, Rhodokanaty's anarchism is firmly rooted in Greek Orthodoxy. Indeed, in a remarkable text published in 1877 in *El Combate* in Mexico, Rhodakanaty mounts a defense of The True Church [*La Verdadera Iglesia*]. I will describe this text in the next section.

While this section has focused on the influence of figures such as Bakunin, Rhodakanaty, and Tolstoy on Latin American anarchism, it would be wrong to limit this presence and influence only to well-known names of anarchism. Equally important to the flourishing of anarchism as a political movement has been the participation of anonymous Orthodox migrants (lay people) in anarchist groups. In the River Plate region from the nineteenth century onward, anarchism was replenished by waves of migration from Europe, including or

Orthodox Europe. The development of anarchist printing presses, the establishment of pamphlets and magazines amongst the urban working classes, and the dissemination (and translation) of anarchist texts from the European movement was taken up by a wide variety of migrants who entered into urban life in Latin America through artisanal jobs like shoemaking, cabinet making, baking, engraving, and so on.[25] In other words, the dissemination of anarchism and its ideas was not restricted to liberal and libertarian Latin American national elites. This observation draws in Orthodoxy, although, at present, it is difficult to find precise sources in the emerging ethnographic material. However, we do know that Orthodox migration to Latin America was largely concentrated in urban centers, we also know that the staging ports for this Orthodox migration were often European ports (where anarchist ideas circulated), and we know that many Orthodox migrants engaged in artisanal trades. Buenos Aries, as the principal city in the River Plate region, is also the location of the oldest Orthodox Church in Latin America.

ANARCHISM AND THE TRUE CHURCH

Anarchism is a minority, yet influential, political movement in Latin America. Anarchism is also a tendency as Davor Džalto helpfully sets out in his book, *Anarchy and the Kingdom of God: From Eschatology to Orthodox Political Theology and Back*. Anarchism as a tendency is understood by Džalto to value freedom, human creativity, and dignity free of coercive power structures.[26] Džalto's book is a theological reflection, or political theology. Rhodokanaty's writings demonstrate that his anarchism is a political theology, deeply rooted in a particular ecclesiological understanding of Orthodoxy. Above all, Rhodokanaty understands anarchism and ecclesiology as love and organized love.

In a short text published in 1877 in Mexico, Rhodokanaty states that the Church is a community established by Christ with the aim of putting into practice the sublime principles of love. He begins by defending "religion" from its critics, advancing the hypothesis that "true religion" is a philosophy the bears the fruits of the beauty of science. He dismisses those who would oppose science and religion. Instead, he embraces scientific advances through an understanding of true religion that "has formulated a vast system of practical truths . . . for all beings of creation."

After setting out the universal scope of "true religion," Rhodokanaty turns to ecclesiological questions. First, he outlines that human beings have real needs and real organization, which are based on love. He interprets this organizational and real need as human solidarity, philanthropy, science, and virtue. Love, as expressed through these concepts, is "capable of the

110 Graham McGeoch

future transfiguring of Humanity," according to Rhodokanaty. This love is also important in countering aspects of modern society where egoism and ignorance disfigure "true religion." At the forefront of egoism and ignorance are sects who would claim for themselves the name of "true religion." Rhodokanaty names Protestantism, Roman Catholicism, and Islam as sects at the forefront of modern egoism and ignorance that wrongly claim to be "true Church."

Rhodokanaty asks, what of those who say they are the true Church? How to distinguish the true Church? Rhodokanaty answers this question by saying it is important to observe, compare, and reason based only on the Gospel and not the romance of the Church. The Gospels warn of false prophets (Matthew 24:11), and Paul's warning that only love counters false prophets must be observed, compared, and reasoned when faced with sects or false religion.

Rhodokanaty's use of Paul will be no surprise to theologians or political theologians. However, he uses a turn of phrase that is perhaps problematic for anarchism. Rhodokanaty outlines his understanding of love, loosely quoting Paul: "Love is patient, love is kind, it does not envy, it is not irrational or boastful. Neither is it hurtful, selfish, angered, or evil minded. Love bears all, and everything grows through it and hopes for it." At the end of this quotation, Rhodokanaty affirms that this description is the best form of religion and in this sense true religion is best understood as "organized love."

"Organized love" counters the sects who proclaim "salvation only by faith" (Protestants). It counters the scholastic syllogisms that obscure scientific advances (Roman Catholicism). It survives the brutal and ferocious invasion of Europe that created Byzantine refugees (Islam). "Organized love," according to Rhodokanaty, finds its best expression in Greek Orthodoxy, the repository of science and the arts and conservers of true Christianity as preached by the apostles. As an example of the "organized love" of Greek Orthodoxy, Rhoodkanaty cites the "spirit of evangelical love" preached from the minarets of Hagia Sofia to the powerful muscovite empire. "Organized love" resists and survives. "The spirit of love is the soul of Christian religion, and this only exists today in the Greek Church."

FINAL REMARKS

The story of anarchism and Orthodox Christianity in Latin America may well be one of a minority presence, but it is a presence nonetheless. The nineteenth and twentieth centuries proved crucial to the "import" of both to the region and the presence of leading anarchists and their relationship to Orthodox Christianity proved influential in shaping the practices of the different tendencies in anarchism in the region. The fact that Bakunin briefly spent time

Anarchism and Orthodoxy in Latin America　　111

in Latin America during his exile is noteworthy. It gives Latin America a direct place within his life and legacy, one that is not only derived from his influential ideas and practices on anarchism more generally. It also introduces antichurch and antireligious positions to emerging anarchism in the region. This anarchist tendency contributed to excluding the Roman Catholic Church from the nation building at the time of independence and was a foil to the rise of nationalist-populist discourses in the early twentieth century.

However, Bakunin's influence must be set alongside other anarchists in the region, particularly Rhodakanaty in Mexico, Tolstoy's literary and artistic influence throughout the region, and later Berydaev's influence on twentieth-century politics and theology in the region, especially under military dictatorships with denied freedom. Rhodakanaty's promotion of a primitive Orthodox Christianity to counter the excessive Enlightenment rationalism of Roman Catholicism and Protestantism in the region offers a significant departure from Bakunin's position, and one that found widespread sympathy with intellectual and political elites keen to curb the power of the institutional Church while preserving their "indigenous" Christianity. Rhodakanaty's vision offered the possibility for a wide range of groups in Latin America to be Christian without the institutional Church, a perspective that continues to prove to be eerily current amongst some Protestant ecclesiologies in the region.

Rhodokanaty's unapologetic defense of the True Church as an "organized love" is a crucial Orthodox ecclesiological contribution to anarchism in Latin America. His defence takes issue with Protestantism, Roman Catholicism, and Islam, and advocates Greek Orthodoxy as the True Church. However, Rhodokanaty's political contribution cannot be overlooked. He wrote the first socialist/anarchist pamphlet in the region, he founded "free schools" on anarchist lines and he stirred up protest and rebellion by peasants and urban working classes alike. His vision of Christian Anarchism is firmly rooted in the Gospels and the theology of love of Paul's texts. And to the consternation of the Roman Catholic bishop, his theological vision is inspired by pantosophic ideas widely in currency in the Orthodoxy of his time.

NOTES

1. Of the four figures mentioned here, Bakunin and Kropotkin are Russian, formed in the cultural milieu of the Russian Orthodox Church, and rejecting the Russian Orthodox Church, although Kropotkin was buried in the family tomb at the Novodevichy Monastery, Moscow.

2. It is worth noting that Benedict Anderson suggests that there are occasions when Anarchism will unite with nationalist anticolonial struggles. See Benedict Anderson,

Under Three Flags: Anarchism and the Anticolonial Imagination (London: Verso, 2005).

3. See Angel. J. Cappelletti, *Anarchism in Latin America* (Edinburgh: AK Press, 2017).

4. Ibid.

5. Luis Martinez Andrade has noted some links between the founding of football clubs and anarchism in Latin America (2022). See Luis Martinez Andrade, *Fútbol y teoria crítica: ilusiones del balón y del sujeto abstracto* (Santander: Editorial La Vorágine, 2022).

6. "Anarcho-bolshevism" has often been a pejorative term applied within anarchism to groups who emphasize organization and discipline. The term often appears in debates (sometimes violent) between liberatarians and authoritarians within anarchism (Evans 2022). Evans notes that Anarcho-bolshevism refers to small groups advocating direct democracy, direct action, and resistance to state legitimacy, including armed resistance. See Danny Evans, "Learning to Live: Anarcho-syndicalism and Utopia in Spain, 1931–37," in *International Journal of Iberian Studies*, vol. 36, no. 1 (2023).

7. See Cappelletti, *Anarchism*.

8. I have written further about this in a special edition journal dedicated to Liberation Christianity and Liberation Theology (McGeoch 2020). See Graham McGeoch, "Liberation Theology: Problematizing the Historical Projects of Democracy and Human Rights," in *Sociedade e Cultura*, vol. 23, p. 1–25 (Gois: Universidade Federal de Gois, 2020)

9. Davor Džalto, *Anarchy and the Kingdom of God: From Eschatology to Orthodox Political Theology and Back* (New York: Fordham University Press, 2021), 9.

10. Cappelletti, *Anarchism*, 351.

11. See Džalto, *Anarchy*, 22.

12. Cappelletti, *Anarchism*, 293.

13. Ibid., 295.

14. See ibid., 295.

15. Rhodokanaty's pantosofic ideas draw on the widely discussed ideas of Vladimir Soloviev (1853–1900). Soloviev's Sophic lectures were first delivered at St Petersburg in 1878, although his ideas quickly spread to other world capitals include Prague, Paris, and Berlin (Kornblatt 2009). See Judith Kornblatt, *Divine Sophia: The Wisdom Writings of Vladimir Solovyov* (Ithaca: Cornell University Press, 2009)

16. Carlos Illades, ed., *Piensamento Socialista del Siglo XIX* (Mexico: UNAM, 2001), 9–10.

17. See Therezinha De Castro, *Historia Documental do Brasil* (Rio de Janeiro: Record, 1968), 45.

18. Ibid., 50.

19. Ibid., 58.

20. Ibid., 59.

21. See Carlos Illades, ed., *Plotino C Rhodokanaty: obras* (Mexico: UNAM, 1998), 21–23.

22. Džalto, *Anarchy*, 123.

Anarchism and Orthodoxy in Latin America 113

23. José Julian Llaguno Thomas, "La Resurrección del Cristo Moderno: Jesús y Tolstoi en las Publicaciones Libertarias em Costa Rica (1904–1914)," in Joel Delhom and Daniel Attala, eds., *Cuando los Anarquistas Citan la Biblia: entre mesianismo e propaganda* (Madrid: Catarata, 2014), 157.

24. In an interesting presentation of the literary (and political) influence of Leo Tolstoy in the region, José Julian Llaguno Thomas points to the intellectuals Gabriel Mistral in Chile, Enrique Nulia in Honduras, and Joaquim Garcia Monge in Costa Rica as important in spreading Tolstoian ideas and practices (Thomas, "La Resurrección," 155).

25. Cappelletti, *Anarchism*, 51.

26. See Džalto, *Anarchism*, 10.

BIBLIOGRAPHY

Anderson, Benedict. *Under Three Flags: Anarchism and the Anticolonial Imagination.* London: Verso, 2005.

Andrade, Luis Martinez. *Fútbol y teoria crítica: ilusiones del balón y del sujeto abstracto.* Santander: Editorial La Vorágine, 2022.

Cappelletti, Angel. J. *Anarchism in Latin America.* Edinburgh: AK Press, 2017.

De Castro, Therezinha. *Historia Documental do Brasil.* Rio de Janeiro: Record, 1968.

Džalto, Davor. *Anarchy and the Kingdom of God: From Eschatology to Orthodox Political Theology and Back.* New York: Fordham University Press, 2021.

Evans, Danny. "Learning to live: Anarcho-syndicalism and utopia in Spain, 1931–37." *International Journal of Iberian Studies*, vol. 36, no. 1 (2023).

Illades, Carlos, ed. *Piensamento Socialista del Siglo XIX.* Mexico: UNAM, 2001.

———. *Plotino C Rhodokanaty: obras.* Mexico: UNAM, 1998.

Kornblatt, Judith Divine Sophia: *The Wisdom Writings of Vladimir Solovyov.* Ithaca: Cornell University Press, 2009.

McGeoch, Graham. "Liberation Theology: problematizing the historical projects of democracy and human rights." In *Sociedade e Cultura*, vol. 23, p. 1–25. Gois: Universidade Federal de Gois, 2020.

Thomas, Julian José Llaguno. "La Resurrección del Cristo Moderno: Jesús y Tolstoi en las Publicaciones Libertarias em Costa Rica (1904–1914)." In *Cuando los Anarquistas Citan la Biblia: entre mesianismo e propaganda*, edited by Joel Delhom and Daniel Attala, 149–68. Madrid: Catarata, 2014.

Chapter 6

Anarchy and Hierarchy

The (Nonoppressive) Holy and the Question of "Spiritual Aristocracy"

Davor Džalto

The concepts of *anarchy/anarchism* and *hierarchy* are often perceived as fundamentally incompatible. There are good reasons for that. Even the etymology of these words suggests an important difference, if not even mutual exclusion. Both "archos" (ἀρχός) and "archon" (ἄρχων) are the Greek words designating the "leader," "ruler," or "commander," and both are etymologically related to "arche" (ἀρχή), which does not only mean "beginning" or "origin," but also "power," "sovereignty," and "authority."[1] "Anarchy" thus indicates a state without the "first" (principle, cause, or ruler), without "rule" or "authority."

Arche is also present in the word "hierarchy" (ἱεραρχία). It means "holy order" or "holy rule" (ἱερός-ἀρχή), that is, the rule of a priest or priests, while the "hierarch" (ἱεράρχης) is the "(high) priest," the one who presides over the sacred rites.[2] In a religious context, the word "hierarchy" does not necessarily imply the existence of a vertical distribution of power, although it is often understood that way.[3] On the contrary, in the common-sense usage of the word, hierarchy primarily implies a pyramidal power structure, where the one on top has most power, which gradually decreases as one moves downward, until one reaches the bottom of the (political, ecclesiastical, corporate . . .) pyramid where one finds those with virtually no power or authority over anybody else, except maybe over one another. Although a pyramidal power structure is not necessarily implied by the word hierarchy, it does imply the existence of some order, and also the existence of the "first" (or "firsts," i.e., elders), who preside(s) over sacred rituals.

115

Fig. 6.1. *A Hierarch on Fire*, ink on paper, 2023. Artist: Davor Džalto

Hierarchy is thus etymologically related not only to "order" and "rule," but specifically to the *sacred, holy* realm, to the things administered by the priests. Of course, in many societies, ancient and modern, the distinction between the "sacred" (religious) and "secular" (political) is not clear, and very often the roles of the religious and secular "hierarchs" merge, so that the chief political figure also functions as the "chief priest," and vice-versa. Thus, the secular-political order, with various social classes, and the sacred-religious order, with its organization, come to be the examples of "hierarchy" in what is now understood as the primary and dominant meaning of the word.

Anarchism, on the other hand, seems to imply exactly the opposite. In more popular understandings of the concept, "anarchy" and "anarchism" stand for chaos, and the political ideology that causes unrest and violence against the established ("God given") order. Many self-designated anarchists have also openly been against any hierarchies, not only state but religious as well. Many have been not only atheists but openly antireligious, seeing in priesthood and organized religion the source of oppression *per se*, and the best allies of dominant (church-state) power structures that provide useful ideological narratives ("the opium of the people") justifying the socio-political order and its oppressiveness, both at the ideological level and at the level of its institutional functioning.

Such positions reveal important truths. From the perspective of the established order and its power structures, every attempt to change that order is normally considered an attempt to bring society into a state of instability and, potentially, into chaos. This is understandable, since those in power can rarely imagine that there can be an order without *them* in the position of power. The current order, in which "we" are "in charge," is thus the *only* possible or, at least, the *best* possible order. Every change is a threat not only to the *current* order, but to the order in principle, with only one possible outcome—chaos and violence. Therefore, a whole range of political systems, from the Liberal-Corporate-Capitalist, via the Conservative-Monarchist or Aristocratic, to the State-Communist, have been the mortal enemies of all of those who aspired to change those systems in order to bring more freedom, justice, and democracy. Those freedom-fighters have routinely been labeled as "anarchists," which the "priestly class" in each society often uses as a synonym for "terrorists."[4]

True, there were also some self-described "anarchists" who can justifiably be labeled as terrorists, who were concerned mostly with how to throw bombs rather than with how to work toward building freer social relations, lowering the amount of oppression in society. The deeds of many of those "anarchists," as Octave Mirbeau put it, were such that "a mortal enemy of anarchism could not have done better."[5]

It is also true that many "hierarchs," traditional priests and ideologists of all kinds, have been diligent in creating power structures and (ideological) narratives that have accompanied those structures, justifying them and rationalizing the need for their existence. Those priests and other ideologists, as well as the political and financial "masters of humankind," have been looking at the established social order (in which they occupy a privileged, "God-given" place) as the most auspicious one. The existing order, in which "we" are in charge (or, at least, close to those in charge, benefiting in some way from the existing order) is the order with a "divine" (or "nature's") approval. There is always something "holy" about the established ideological-political-economic system, either in some traditional-religious understanding of the sacred, or in the sense of modern secular (civil) religious "sacredness."[6] The dominant order is always supplied by a "sacred" aura. This can be seen across various systems, from ancient Egyptian society, Islamic caliphates and medieval Western "sacred monarchies," to modern "Liberal Democracies," where the dominant ideological discourse, with its corresponding financial power structures and a certain sense of duty and morality, is understood as sacrosanct. The perception of the sacredness of the prevalent social order normally operates at a deeper, subconscious level, and exists even when a certain level of cynicism is allowed to penetrate the mainstream public discourse (e.g., when there is a talk of our "purely technocratic" governments, incapable of doing their job). Of course, there is the role of private interests, power games, and manipulations where the slogans about "patriotism," "morality," or "our (sacred) democracy" are used as effective propaganda instruments for power and money gains. However, even this purely instrumental reference to some "higher" values that are supposed to constitute the polity can work and be effective only because of their reliance on the presupposed secular-religious sentiment that many, if not most people, sympathize with. The absorbed, interiorized sense of the sacrosanct character of the socio-political-ideological sphere (typical of [Post]Protestant/Liberal ideology) is revealed whenever the questioning of systemic injustices, oppression, and evil that is done within the dominant epistemic and institutional horizon is perceived as a dangerous activity, which is rejected and condemned in the public realm (using propaganda machinery), in the name of the affirmation of the status quo and the belief that, somehow, despite slight imperfections that the dominant order may exhibit here and there, the system as such is good and just, and its meaning should not be questioned. The "heretics," those disturbing the (desired) quiet waters of the existing "holy order," may not necessarily be roasted at the stake nowadays; they can also be effectively marginalized, thrown out of their jobs, subjected to defamatory campaigns and media witch hunts, and their property confiscated. If they do not reconcile with the sociopolitical whole, through repentance, and continue demonstrating stubbornness rejecting to conform to the dominant ideological discourse, they will be thrown

Anarchy and Hierarchy 119

into prison cells where they can be kept indefinitely, or tortured in the name of freedom, democracy, and morality.

Those opposing the existing order are perceived as dangerous "trouble-makers" for a good reason—those oppressed, or those who argue for the abolishment of oppression (even if they are not directly affected by it) would often prefer "more chaos" rather than the *status quo*, which means the indefinite perpetuation of oppression. Shaking the shackles can create an opportunity, or, at least, give a hope that the shackles will eventually fall off. As I claimed elsewhere, sometimes we gain more freedom by destroying a system, while at other times, and under different circumstances, more freedom is gained by establishing a system.[7] If we are genuinely interested in anarchism as a way of expanding the horizons of freedom and justice, we need to think and act contextually, never rigidly, never automatically applying simple, fixed, ready-made dogmas to complex social realities.

Does this mean that anarchy and anarchists are necessarily the enemies of every hierarchy and hierarchs, and vice versa? Is there a way to reconcile anarchism and hierarchy, without sacrificing the emancipatory dimension in anarchism? Does every attempt to establish bridges between the two necessarily leads into the corruption of anarchism and its causes, blunting the blade of the anarchist critique, ending up in social conformity and the perpetuation of the status quo in which yesterday's anarchist would be today's "priests," co-opted by the system, integrated into a modified version of the same? I do not think this is inevitable.

DEFINING ANARCHY
(WHILE DEFYING THE DEFINITION)

"Anarchy" and "anarchism," just as "democracy" or "communism," have been used in such a variety of ways that there is little point in discussing them without a prior clarification of what one means by them. This is often more difficult than it seems. On the one hand, one should not use these terms in a completely arbitrary way, which would just add to the confusion that is already there. On the other hand, however, one cannot simply adopt the dominant, popular (often prereflexive) way of using these terms either, since, more often than not, such usage operates at the level of propaganda narratives, without any deeper foundation. By simply adopting popular understandings constructed through the propaganda industry, the meanings that reflect ideological narratives and interests of the engineers of the "public opinion" would be imported, and thus any potentially subversive content present in these concepts would also be effectively neutralized. The engineers of the "public opinion" do not even need to be old-fashioned individuals or institutions;

algorithms are increasingly being used to that effect, operating, of course, within the pregiven ideological paradigms. The task then requires that some of these key terms are defined in specific, sometimes even "eccentric" ways that, however, would not be arbitrary, but rooted in some of the obscured and often intentionally marginalized histories.

I understand anarchism primarily as a *method*. It refers to the skepticism toward power structures; it requires a constant critical examination of those structures and the way they operate. Anarchism stands for an active opposition to every illegitimate exercise of power and authority, to every oppression and injustice, in the name of the affirmation of human freedom and dignity.[8]

In this sense, anarchism is against "rule" and dominant "orders," but not in order to destroy them for the sake of destroying them; it is against dominant ideological systems and the oppression they produce in the name of the expansion of the horizon of human freedom and justice. Anarchism values human beings, together with other beings in this world. In the terminology of Christian theology, anarchists value the entirety of God's creation. Anarchists oppose oppression, cruelty, torture, killing, or any other illegitimate exercise of power and authority, whether it comes from large-scale systems and institutions (e.g., states, multinational corporations) or from individuals. This opposition is a matter of principle.[9]

Understood this way, anarchism does not advocate one specific program or one "ideal" system in order to achieve optimal social conditions. It does not propose a "manual" for how to organize human societies in all historical periods, disregarding the specificities of each context. Anarchism opposes oppression, in the name of human dignity, freedom, justice, and well-being, and it advocates this for all human beings, but how this opposition is manifested in concrete societies and historical periods depends on those social and historical circumstances and the people who live in them. It is always different. It is a grave danger to petrify one model, one value system or ethical code, and apply it dogmatically regardless of the local context. Different societies work differently, different people and their local communities have different experiences and histories, different understandings of what constitutes a value, what's the priority, and so on. A violent imposition of certain "agendas," a dogmatic belief that "our" political model and "our way of life" are the best and most emancipatory, and that they should, as such, be universally applied—is a source of oppression, not liberation. History is full of examples of such self-righteous and self-appointed promoters of particular "progressive" and "enlightened" agendas, whose (passive) aggressive certitude and the bankrupt intellectual conformity have produced a number of major ideological blind spots. For example, many of the mainstream North American Liberals, who advocate for "bringing democracy and human rights" by military interventions or sanctions, are not simply hypocrites, who repeat

Anarchy and Hierarchy 121

this propaganda narrative to cover up what's really going on (and that is the imperial wars for the control over strategically important territories and their natural resources, plus the big money the corporate sector can make out of those wars). Many of them are simply too indoctrinated so that they actually believe that "bringing democracy and human rights"—by destroying entire regions, killing and torturing people, or turning them into refugees—is a way to bring more freedom and justice. Similarly, to the earlier religious missionaries, these secular-religious missionaries advance their dogmas according to which only one model (namely "ours") is the right one, so everybody else better conform to that standard, if they aspire to be saved.

On the other hand, however, I do not think that anarchists, if they understand anarchism as a method and not as a fixed doctrine, need to refrain from having any contact with institutions that have a certain hierarchical organization (e.g., churches, universities, states). Under concrete circumstances, cooperation with ecclesiastical structures or democratized state institutions can be a much more meaningful strategy to arrive at the maximization of freedom and well-being in a concrete context, and at that particular time, then trying to simply get rid of them, which (in concrete situations) can easily be counterproductive, leading to more oppression. This, of course, is the question of strategy and tactics, not principles. If one cooperates with such institutions, provided that such cooperation is justified by the circumstances (and not motivated by private profits or career goals), it does not mean that one supports the power structures that exist in those institutions; it only means that disregarding concrete social conditions, with its limitations and opportunities, may very easily lead into impotence or, worse, into an active complacency in the oppression. This also means that the support for particular programs or political actions—at the level of strategy and tactics—is very much needed; again, not because of the belief that one particular program or action represents the embodiment of anarchist ideals, a prescription for a universal solution everywhere and at all times, but because one judges that those actions, here and now, are the best way to fight against the most acute types of oppression and injustice around us.

Anarchism as a method reminds us that there is always something *wrong* with societies in which we live, there are always ideological blind spots that need to be critically examined. No normality is satisfactory in the long run; as soon as a normality is established, anarchists should examine it critically, offer different, unusual perspectives and counterexamples, in order to arrive at constructive suggestions for how to change things, or think about them differently. That is why we need, to paraphrase Yevgeny Zamyatin, "madmen, hermits, heretics, dreamers, rebels, and skeptics," not only to sustain "true literature" but also to make our societies more humane. It is true that societies composed mostly of madmen, hermits, heretics, dreamers, rebels, and skeptics would probably not be the most pleasant societies to live in, but it is also true that "perfect societies," without those labeled as "madmen," "heretics," or "rebels," would be the most totalitarian and oppressive societies that human history has seen.

(UN)HOLY HIERARCHIES

If we use the concept of anarchism in the above explained sense, it is clear that hierarchies understood as power structures, with a vertical/pyramidal distribution of power (whether they appear in social-political, ecclesiastical, business, or any other type of entities), are, from an anarchist perspective, problematic in principle. Those structures, even if they are not actively oppressing the subordinated, have an oppressive potential, and emancipation can consist already in raising the awareness of that potential. These are the *evil hierarchies*, that reflect the *evilness* of the necessity attached to the logic of our historical existence.[10]

However, as we have seen, *hierarchy* can also be understood as "sacred order," where the purpose of its existence is not to exercise power, or administer its distribution, but to provide the possibility of an "upward" movement, enabling a gradual access to *holy things* that bring the quality of *holiness* within the ordinary "here" and "now." In a Christian perspective, this holiness is a manifestation of the presence of the Holy Spirit, or, to put it differently, it is the manifestation of the *eschaton* in the course of history, the manifestation of the presence of the Kingdom of God already "here" and "now."

Of course, it is understood that this administration of the things holy can easily get confused with the exercise of power (as it usually does). Those who perform sacred rituals on behalf of the congregation are normally those who also enjoy various privileges outside of the realm of sacred rites. Where there is a more complex hierarchical system, with "upper" and "lower" echelons of priests (that are related to the various levels of their access to the holy), the administrative, political, and financial power of the priestly class often reflects those hierarchies. This, regardless of how often it appears, can be considered a corruption of something that does not need to be seen as being necessarily tied to *evil hierarchies*.

This (nonevil) hierarchy, as the nonoppressive administration of holy things, is closely linked to *mystical ascension*. In fact, the sole purpose of the existence of true hierarchy is to allow for the mystical ascension, for the union between the holy (the eschatological) and the created world (history). The concept of mystical ascension can, of course, be found across different religious traditions. In the context of Judeo-Christianity, we find

Anarchy and Hierarchy											123

its paradigmatic expression in the function and structure of the Tent of the Covenant, or (with the same basic structure) in the Temple of Jerusalem.

The prototype for how to build the Tent was shown to Moses on Mount Sinai, which means that the Tent/Temple was the image of the prototype seen "above," in a "high place." Since climbing up a mountain often figures as an icon of a spiritual ascent, this imagery has been interpreted in the Christian tradition as the ascent into the *presence of God*, into the (true) "holy of holies," the "place" where God Himself abides (i.e., the eschaton). In this case, Mount Sinai acquires a more specific eschatological dimension since it was absorbed within the cloud of God's glory.[11] God "descended" on the mountain, which also means that the mountain (or those on the mountain, i.e., Moses) "ascended" into the presence of God, glimpsing into eternity (the eschaton), *behind the veil* of history and matter.[12]

The prototype for the place of worship—the Tent/Temple—is thus an eschatological one, received in the presence of God. What happens there has eschatological consequences and represents a manifestation of the future Kingdom of God. However, what happens in the Tent/Temple is also never fully completed within history; it is fulfilled only in the eschaton. The mystical ascension is thus *iconized* in spatial as well as in temporal categories; what is physically "above" symbolizes the (meta)temporal aspect, the "fullness of time," which, in that sense, stands "above" the regular flow of the historical time. The logic of the mystical/spiritual ascent means that sacred things are received from "above," from a "high place," again as an indication of their eschatological (i.e., extra- or supra-worldly/temporal) origin. We can see this logic in the way the Tent/Temple of Jerusalem "worked."

The Tent/Temple consisted of the fenced courtyard which already suggested a degree of exclusivity—the holy was housed within an enclosed area. The fence separated the holy ground on which the tent/temple sat from the ordinary world. Indeed, sacrifices were offered in the courtyard, and ritual cleansings were also performed there. Within the courtyard stood the Tent/Temple consisting of two rooms. The first was bigger; it was the "holy place." The holy place was accessible only to the priests. From the holy place one could enter the smaller room, the "holy of holies" (or the "most holy place"), which was accessible only to the high priest. The holy of holies was behind the veil, which made its interior invisible from the holy place, and it was also elevated relative to the holy place. This progressive exclusivity of the place is directly proportional to the "levels" of holiness. The more exclusive— the holier.

"High places" in many ancient religious traditions, including the Hebrew, signify sacred places, where sacrifices were offered. Thus, the "high place" of Jerusalem also refers to the Temple of Jerusalem (see 1 Samuel 9:12–10:13), while another indication of elevation, "from above," is used in some cases to

124   *Davor Džalto*

refer to the holy of holies, the dwelling place of God (on Earth) (see Ezekiel 10:4; 10:18). The holy of holies symbolized eternity, the realm of the Divine presence. It was thus the (conceptual) "center" of the Temple, the most *elevated* part, both in terms of its holiness and its physical position relative to the rest of the Temple (notice that the Temple building was also elevated relative to the courtyard, just as the Temple Mount was elevated relative to the rest of the city).

The sacredness stemming from the presence of God (i.e., from one's presence in the presence of God in the holy of holies, as an icon of eternity) is administered by the high priest, who, by entering the holy of holies, exits the space-time as we know it, and becomes an *angel* of God, that is, a *deified* human. Upon exiting the holy of holies, the high priest would go through the veil, symbolizing the created world. In the figure of the high priest we can see the image of Godman (the future Messiah), since the high priest was a human who, by the virtue of his presence in the presence of God, also became divine.

Hierarchy here is linked with the administration of Divine gifts, and the duty of *purifying* the world, *transforming* it, making it *holy*. A complex symbolism, which we find in the words/concepts used in the rituals, in the spatial logic of the place, in visual, tactile, acoustic as well as olfactory sensations, in the liturgical vestments and actions performed, is there to enable a *communion* between the radically *other* (God) and the world. The elevation (physical and symbolic) stands for the exclusivity, which itself symbolizes the importance and uniqueness of the sacred. The "high place" is a symbol of the mystical (spiritual/eschatological) ascent. The movement toward the things that are from "above" is thus there to prevent trivialization, to facilitate the process of *transfiguration*, which leads to the communion with God. Ultimately, it is a symbol of deification, of the *ascendence* from the natural state into the deified state. This ascendence requires an *immersion* into the natural (material), not an escape from it. The hierarch (priest) is thus the one who iconizes Christ, the incarnate God.[13]

Nikolai Berdyaev sheds additional light on the question of hierarchy, with his concept of "spiritual aristocracy." For Berdyaev, "Every vital level—is hierarchical and has its own aristocracy, non-hierarchical only is the pile of dust and only in it is there not separated out any sort of aristocratic qualifications."[14] Hierarchy and aristocracy (as an expression of "true" hierarchy) have to do with principles and existential attitudes so to speak, and not so much with historical realities, where these principles are often confused or perverted: "Aristocracy as regards its very idea—is sacrificial. But it can betray its idea."[15] This is the reason why Berdyaev makes a clear distinction between "true hierarchy" and "true aristocracy," and "false hierarchies" and "false aristocracies." A proper "aristocratic hierarchy" often degenerates into

Anarchy and Hierarchy   125

an "ochlocratic hierarchy."[16] In the Christian context, "the toppling of the hierarchy of Christ creates the hierarchy of the Anti-Christ."[17]

In his understanding of (proper, true) hierarchy, Berdyaev affirms its etymological meaning, as something that is intrinsically connected with the Divine, and the sacred.[18] There is something *spiritual* in the aristocratic principle that, for Berdyaev, makes it Christian in a profound sense. If that is missing, aristocracy cannot be justified. Berdyaev does not speak here of aristocracy as a ruling class, with inherited privileges acquired by birth. In order to differentiate these two meanings of aristocracy, he speaks of "spiritual aristocracy," which is not defined by birth, origin, material wealth, or one's class. He warns against the confusion between "a spiritual aristocracy and the "historical aristocracy":

> No one, certainly, should tend to confuse and regard as identical a spiritual aristocracy with the historical aristocracy. The representatives of the historical aristocracy can stand quite low in the spiritual regard, and the very utmost representatives of a spiritual aristocracy cannot emerge and even usually do not emerge from the aristocratic strata. This is—indisputable and elementary.[19]

A key characteristic of *true, spiritual* aristocracy is generosity: "Proper to aristocratism—is generosity, and not greed. True aristocracy can serve others, can serve man and the world, since it is not concerned with self-advancement, for to begin with it stands sufficiently high. It is—sacrificial."[20] Thus, generosity acquires a religious, metaphysical significance. It is a sign that one has liberated him/herself from the slavery imposed on us by the logic of "this world." In this sense, Christianity, for Berdyaev, is "an aristocratic religion, a religion of free sons of God, a religion of the gifted grace of God."[21] There is nothing more alien to this "spiritual aristocracy" than the struggle for power, wealth, or special (private) interest—such struggle is "by nature non-aristocratic."[22]

"Spiritual aristocracy" is also "esoteric," "the domain of the saints or holy elders represents the esoteric religious aristocracy," which should, again, be differentiated from "exoteric aristocracy," as the "outwardly legitimate historical churchly hierarchy."[23]

Spiritual aristocracy thus implies the principle according to which the human *person* is manifested in the world, being born "from above," that is from the heavenly sphere, the eschaton. This makes the human person free from the necessities attached to the biological birth and procreation, or the necessities attached to one's rank in society or one's economic standing. This freedom, and the dignity that the person acquires from its "spiritual birth" so to say, enables the person to act in history in a generous, selfless, and even a self-sacrificial manner. The meaning of the true hierarchy is, thus, revealed

126 *Davor Džalto*

in one's service to others, and to the whole world, quite in line with Christ's instructions to those who want to be "the first":

> You know that those who are regarded as rulers of the Gentiles lord it over them, and their high officials exercise authority over them. Not so with you. Instead, whoever wants to become great among you must be your servant, and whoever wants to be first must be slave of all. For even the Son of Man did not come to be served, but to serve, and to give his life as a ransom for many. (Mark 10:42–45)

This hierarchy is not a hierarchy of power and oppression, but rather a *sacred service*, offered out of love, whose purpose is to liberate humans and the world from the slavery to the (necessity of the) world, and our own (biological, historical, social) *self*. Berdyaev's "spiritual aristocracy" is not a secular category, it is not a noble ideal for the organization of society, and it is especially not a selected group of people of higher (socioeconomic or moral) standing working toward making the world a "better place." This "spiritual aristocracy" is there to help lift the world up, to the greater proximity of the "high place," to the "holy of holies," that is to the Kingdom of God itself. It is *hierarchic* in the sense that it performs a priestly role, it administers "holy things," offering sacrifices (including one's own life) to God, for others, and for the transfiguration of the world (in which the world finds its salvation).

Understood this way, the concept of "spiritual aristocracy" becomes quite compatible with the anarchist method as it was defined above.

Berdyaev's attitude toward anarchism seems ambivalent, and a superficial reading of various texts, from different periods, could produce an impression that he, paradoxically, both elevates it and criticizes it in very harsh terms.

In "Concerning Anarchism," Berdyaev writes about revolutionary anarchists whom he characterizes as "spiritually proletarian,"[24] a concept that apparently mirrors "spiritual aristocracy" as its (negative) counterpart. Anarchism thus stands for:

> [A]n atomism, the disintegration of all the societal totalities into self-asserting atoms . . . The triumph of anarchism would be the falling apart of all the hierarchies of reality, of the organic connections between them, the destruction of all cosmic order, the revolt of chaos against cosmos . . . Into the chaotic darkness they [cosmic realities] would be submerged, and the chaotic darkness would be admitted the sole reality.[25]

Berdyaev also accuses anarchists of enslaving the human being, while claiming that they are setting humans free: "You anarchists set no one free. It is not man that you set free, but rather you set free chaotic non-being, in which man perishes. [. . .] [A]narchism does not liberate man, rather it enslaves him all

Anarchy and Hierarchy 127

the more. [. . .] A truly free spirit cannot be an anarchist, in having no one and nothing to overthrow. The anarchist mindset—is the mindset of the slave."[26]

This criticism had been outlined in his earlier work as well (in *The New Religious Consciousness and Society*, from 1907). Both in his 1907 and 1923 texts, Berdyaev discusses anarchists such as Mikhail Bakunin and Max Stierner, but also Proudhon and Leo Tolstoy. He shows most sympathies for Tolstoy, who, in Berdyaev's view, "is not a vulgar political revolutionary," and reveals the "religious roots of anarchism."[27] Berdyaev credits Tolstoy for his ability to criticize (the historical forms of) anarchism, for showing that "anarchism is impossible not only on the basis of positivism and atheism, but also on the basis of rationalistic and moralistic Christianity."[28]

What is revealed here is that Berdyaev's criticism of anarchism is, in fact, the criticism of the dominant historical manifestations of anarchism. These manifestations (in, for instance, Bakunin or Stierner) are rooted in a rationalistic positivism,[29] which Berdyaev rejects. However, Berdyaev has all the sympathies for anarchism as a religiously grounded political philosophy. This anarchism takes into account the need for the transfiguration of human nature, which historical forms of anarchism deny: "Anarchism sees absolutely to set man free, without having changed and transformed his nature, leaving him a slave of sin and passions. It desires a realm of freedom without redemption."[30]

The (religious) attempt to liberate the human being from slavery in the metaphysical realm, and not just in the sociopolitical one, leads to a *theocratic anarchism*, since only "theocracy can unite perfect socialism, as a form of social contract, with perfect anarchism, which implies the liberation of the human person from every authority," and results in a "mystical revolution."[31] Consistent anarchism, the one which "negates every state power and every violence, regardless of their origin," unites all people; it is based on "free love," and it opts for "theocracy."[32] "Theocratic anarchism" is the path of resistance to every statism, every political organization (including the one which would be administered by priests) based on power and oppression. A "healthy anarchism" leads to a gradual development and perfection of society, and it is reflected in the decentralization of government, in the development of self-managing communities, and the development of federalism.[33]

In a couple of later writings Berdyaev returned to the issue of anarchism. The meaning of the concept of "theocratic anarchism" is there revealed, I think, more clearly than before, when he writes:

> The religious truth of anarchism consists in this, that power over man is bound up with sin and evil, that a state of perfection is a state where there is no power of man over man, that is to say, anarchy. The Kingdom of God is freedom and the absence of such power; no categories of the exercise of such power are to

be transferred to it. The Kingdom of God is anarchy. This is truth of aphophatic theology; the religious truth of anarchism is a truth of apophatics.[34]

The problem of the political—which is intimately related to power and oppression—can thus only be successfully resolved metaphysically.

SPIRITUAL ARISTOCRACY AND THEOCRATIC ANARCHISM

Berdyaev's concepts of "spiritual aristocracy" and "theocratic anarchism" are both rooted in his major concern—for human freedom. "Spiritual aristocracy" symbolizes the movement upward, toward the realm of the Spirit (the Divine), and in that sense it also stands for the liberated humanity, for those who embrace their freedom, which ultimately manifests itself in self-sacrificial love. Quite compatible with that, "theocratic anarchism" denies legitimacy to any earthly form of government (including "Christian states" or *theocracies* understood as the rule of the priestly class, or God's "representatives" on Earth), as they all manifest various degrees of oppression. "Theocratic anarchism" reveals that the question of political organization is metaphysically rooted, that the problem of oppression cannot fully and successfully be resolved in the socio-political realm, but in the eschaton. However, in the Kingdom of God, there is no "rule," it is "anarchy" as a state of freedom, where personal relationships are based on freedom and love. There and then, all are gathered in and around Christ, as the Great High Priest, who presides over the (eternal) Eucharistic gathering.

In his works, Berdyaev was not focused on liturgy as a manifestation of *eschatological anarchy* in history. And yet, following Orthodox Eucharistic theology, liturgy is a prefiguration of the Kingdom of God, where the "icon of Christ" (the High Priest presiding over the Eucharistic gathering) offers the Eucharistic sacrifice on behalf of all those who are gathered at the liturgical celebration, but also on behalf of all humankind and the entirety of God's creation. Liturgy, just as its prototype—the eschatological Kingdom of God—is *hierarchical* in the original meaning of the word; there is a "sacred order," administered by the priests, i.e., the hierophants (ἱεροφάντης), those *revealing* sacred things. However, this order *is not* (meaning, it *should not be*) hierarchical in the sense of the false hierarchies or the "pyramid of power," with various levels of (potential or real) oppression attached to it. It is hierarchical in the sense that holy mysteries are distributed from the "high place," and the entirety of the world is brought into the presence of the One who sits in the "high place," for the transfiguration/consecration of the faithful and the world. The position of the "first" (who is the "last," the servant of all) is

Anarchy and Hierarchy 129

supposed to be sustained by the love and approval of others, who are "one" with Christ through the iconic role of the "first," as the image of Christ in this world. Everyone "below" the "first one" (Christ) is *equal* in "rank," in the sense that they are all brothers and sisters. Their mutual relationships are supposed to be based primarily on love. As equal, they all serve one another, as the children of the Heavenly Father (who is "above"). The earthly priest iconizes the eternal High Priest, in whom all become One, united in love. The earthly high priest enters into the "holy of holies" (the eschaton) on behalf of everyone, and distributes the Divine gifts that transform all of the members of the liturgical gathering into *angels* (*gods*).[35]

True hierarchy and *true* anarchy are thus intimately linked. The role of the one who presides over the liturgical gathering, insofar as it iconizes Christ, is a position of service, not power. It is rooted in Christ's sacrifice for others. It is also a reminder that in the Kingdom of God, Christ will be that high priest who will be, eternally, offering Himself (i.e., His love) as the (spiritual) food and drink which will be sustaining the life of His *angels* (divinized humans) without an end.

Iconizing the incarnate God, the hierarch performs a *hierophany* as an act of *showing the sacred*, that is, an act of *iconization*. Thus, the Kingdom becomes present in history, and the world becomes present in the holy of holies (the eschaton). Hierarchy becomes a way to put things into the *right* (eschatological) perspective, to point to a path toward the Kingdom, in which worldly hierarchy dissolves. *True hierarchy* thus leads into—anarchy. A true hierarchy (on earth) works toward its own *annihilation*, so to speak, by the transformation of the world which allows for a full presence of the Kingdom, in which all existence will be *made* out of the ontically real "stuff"—freedom and love.

Understanding liturgical hierarchy this way, we also notice that it lacks a "pyramidal" organization, as a series of various ranks whose importance is directly proportional to their proximity to the "top," while the number of those belonging to particular ranks typically increases with the decrease of the rank's importance. The fact that the institutional church evolved precisely that way, mirroring political structures, obscured the basic significance of hierarchy understood as the liturgical service. The "one" is the icon of Christ offering the eucharistic sacrifice, and all are united in their "first," which means that there cannot be any other "ones" or "firsts." The presence of the "one"—the high priest who presides over the liturgical gathering and who iconizes Christ—and "angels," understood properly, eliminates various "ranks" within the liturgical hierarchy. In other words, there is only one "first," and the rest are "equals" as they are all priests, by baptism, by their embrace of the new (eschatological) existence. When the "first" is not there, then someone else (one of the "angels") effectively becomes the one (the "first") presiding over the liturgical gathering. Everyone else is united with this "one/first," iconizing the Kingdom of God, where "many will be one" and "one—many." Through the one/first, who *is* (the icon of) Christ, all become members of the mystical body of Christ (Church). All born from the Spirit, in the eschaton, are brothers and sisters who are gathered around Christ, all of them being *equal* in their self-sacrificial love. No "ranks" are possible, and there cannot be any power distribution based on various "levels" of proximity to the "first." This is the basic and anarchic structure of the liturgical gathering, which mirrors the Kingdom of God—the true anarchy.

NOTES

1. See these terms in *LSJ—Ancient Greek Dictionaries*: https://lsj.gr/wiki/%E1%BC%80%CF%81%CF%87%CF%8C%CF%82 https://lsj.gr/wiki/%E1%BC%84%CF%81%CF%87%CF%89%CE%BD https://lsj.gr/wiki/%E1%BC%80%CF%81%CF%87%CE%AE, as well as in *Etymology Online*: https://www.etymonline.com/word/archon?ref=etymonline_crossreference.

2. *Morphologia Graeca* defines ἱεράρχᾱς and ἱεράρχης as the "president of sacred rites"; see https://morphologia_gr_en.en-academic.com/808140/ἱεράρχᾱς.

3. This is, in fact, the primary meaning of the word according to the Merriam-Webster Dictionary of the English language: hierarchy is "a ruling body of clergy organized into orders or ranks each subordinate to the one above it especially: the bishops of a province or nation [. . .] the classification of a group of people according to ability or to economic, social, or professional standing [. . .] a graded or ranked series." See: https://www.merriam-webster.com/dictionary/hierarchy.

4. Compare with Errico Malatesta's important remark: "In those epochs and countries where people have considered government by one man (monarchy) necessary, the word *republic* (that is, government of many) has been used precisely like Anarchy, to imply disorder and confusion." Errico Malatesta, "Anarchy," in *Patterns of Anarchy: A Collection of Writings on the Anarchist Tradition*, eds. Leonard I. Krimerman and Lewis Perry (New York: Anchor Books, 1966), 2.

5. Quoted in: Noam Chomsky, *On Anarchism* (London: Penguin, 2014), 1.

6. See Emilio Gentile, *Politics as Religion*, trans. George Staunton (Princeton, NJ: Princeton University Press, 2006).

7. See Davor Džalto, *Anarchy and the Kingdom of God: From Eschatology to Orthodox Christian Political Theology and Back* (New York: Fordham University Press, 2021), 252.

8. For a more detailed discussion on the concept of anarchism, the way I understand it, see ibid., 7–24.

9. This definition is close to the one given by Derry Novak: "The essence of anarchist thought is the emphasis of the freedom of the individual, leading to the denial and condemnation of any authority which hinders his free and full development, particularly the State. The rejection of all authority represents the main contribution

of anarchism to political thought and distinguishes it from other political and social theories some of which, for example, liberalism, may have other features similar to anarchism, and may even start from the same basis." Derry Novak, "The Place of Anarchism in the History of Political Thought," in *Patterns of Anarchy*, 6. Novak's emphasis on individualism and antistatist approach as crucial for anarchism need to be understood within the context in which his reflections were written (1958), and the primary issues of the post-WWII faced, with the predominance of liberalism on the one side, and the "red empire" (the Soviet Union) on the other, which claimed to be "leftist" and "socialist/communist" in its character. My definition of anarchism is, however, broader. First of all, I want to acknowledge that states ceased to be the only super-power terrorizing human beings, and that in addition to state violence we also have multinational corporations, some of which have become much more powerful than many individual states. Second, I do not insist only on individualism, since I understand that the ideology of individualism can be as oppressive and enslaving as the ideology of collectivism. So individual freedoms need to be seen within society and social relations, and not always against it (except when society exercises illegitimate oppression against individuals). In this sense, my approach is also much more contextual.

10. The disintegration of the created world in its historical existence is best illustrated by Berdyaev's understanding of time. He uses the terms of "false time" and "evil time" (apparently as synonyms) to point to the *bad endlessness* of the creaturely existence in history, as opposed to the endlessness of the eschatological existence. See Nikolai Berdyaev, *The Meaning of History*, trans. George Reavy (London: Lowe and Brydone, 1949), 64–66, 70; for the discussion about creation, time, and eschatology, based on Berdyaev, see also Davor Džalto, *The Human Work of Art: A Theological Appraisal of Creativity and the Death of the Artist* (Yonkers, NY: SVS Press, 2014), 104–25.

11. "On the morning of the third day there was thunder and lightning. A cloud covered the mountain, and a very loud horn sounded. All the people among the tents shook with fear. Then Moses brought the people from among the tents to meet God. They stood at the base of the mountain. Mount Sinai was all in smoke because the Lord came down upon it in fire. Its smoke went up like the smoke of a stove. And the whole mountain shook. The sound of the horn became louder and louder. Moses spoke, and God answered him with thunder. Then the Lord came down upon Mount Sinai, to the top of the mountain. The Lord called Moses to the top of the mountain, and he went up" (Exodus 19:16–20). See also: "Then Moses went up with Aaron, Nadab, Abihu and seventy of the leaders of Israel. And they saw the God of Israel. The ground under His feet looked like sapphire stone, as clear as the sky itself. He did not let His hand come against the leaders of Israel. But they saw God, and ate and drank" (Exodus 24:9–11). "Then Moses went up on the mountain, which was covered with a cloud. The shining-greatness of the Lord rested on Mount Sinai. And the cloud covered it for six days. On the seventh day He called to Moses from the cloud. To the people of Israel, the shining-greatness of the Lord looked like a fire that destroys on the mountain top. Moses went into the cloud as he went up on the mountain. And Moses was on the mountain forty days and forty nights" (Exodus 24:15–18).

132   *Davor Džalto*

12. Vladimir Lossky refers to this in his *The Mystical Theology of the Eastern Church*: "It is then that he hears 'the many notes of the trumpets, he sees the many lights which flash forth many pure rays; then he is separated from the many, and with the chosen priests he reaches the height of the divine ascents. Even here he does not associate with God, he does not contemplate God (for He is unseen), but the place where He is. I think this means that the highest and most divine of the things which are seen and understood are a kind of hypothetical account of what is subject to Him who is over all. Through them is revealed the presence of Him who is above all thought, a presence which occupies the intelligible heights of His holy places. It is then that Moses is freed from the things that see and are seen (τῶν ὁρωμένων καὶ τῶν ὁρώντων): he passes into the truly mystical darkness of ignorance, where he shuts his eyes to all scientific apprehensions, and reaches what is entirely untouched and unseen, belonging not to himself and not to another, but wholly to Him who is above all. He is united to the best of his powers with the unknowing quiescence of all knowledge, and by that very unknowing he knows what surpasses understanding (καὶ τῷ μηδὲν γινώσκειν, ὑπὲρ νοῦν γινώσκων).' [. . .] St. Gregory Nazianzen takes up the same images, especially that of Moses. 'I was running,' he says, 'to lay hold on God, and thus I went up into the mount, and drew aside the curtain of the cloud, and entered away from matter and from material things, and as far as I could I withdrew within myself. And then when I looked up, I scarce saw the back parts of God; although I was sheltered by the Rock, the Word that was made flesh for us. And when I looked a little closer, I saw, not the first and unmingled nature, known to itself—to the Trinity, I mean; not that which abideth within the first veil, and is hidden by the Cherubim; but only that nature, which at last even reaches to us. And that, so far as I can learn, is the majesty, or as holy David calls it, the glory, which is manifested amongst creatures.'" Vladimir Lossky, *The Mystical Theology of the Eastern Church* (Crestwood, NY: SVS Press, 1997), 27–28, 35–36.

13. The understanding of the purpose of hierarchy along the lines of mystical ascent we find in the *Corpus Areopagiticum*. In *Ecclesiastical Hierarchy*, we find the following explanation of hierarchy: " . . . the Hierarch himself, according to his essence, and analogy, and rank, is initiated in Divine things, and is deified and imparts to the subordinates, according to the meetness of each for the sacred deification which comes to him from God; also that the subordinates follow the superior, and elevate the inferior towards things in advance; and that some go before, and, as far as possible, give the lead to others; and that each, as far as may be, participates in the truly Beautiful, and Wise, and Good, through this the inspired and sacerdotal harmony. [. . .] Now the assimilation to, and union with, God, as far as attainable, is deification. And this is the common goal of every Hierarchy,—the clinging love towards God and Divine things divinely and uniformly ministered; and previous to this, the complete and unswerving removal of things contrary, the knowledge of things as they are in themselves; the vision and science of sacred truth; the inspired communication of the uniform perfection of the One Itself, as far as attainable; the banquet of contemplation, nourishing intelligibly, and deifying every man elevated towards it." Cap. I, sec. II and III.

Anarchy and Hierarchy

14. Nikolas Berdyaev, *The Philosophy of Inequality: Letters to My Contemners, Concerning Social Philosophy*, trans. Stephen Janos (Mohrsville, PA: Frsj Publications, 2016 [1923]), 123.

15. Berdyaev, *Inequality*, 128.

16. See ibid., 123.

17. Ibid.

18. "Aristocracy was created by God and from God it receives its qualities." Berdyaev, *Inequality*, 124.

19. Ibid., 129.

20. Ibid., 124.

21. Ibid., 126.

22. Ibid., 128.

23. Ibid., 135–36. Berdyaev, however, recognizes the importance of the existence of this "exoteric" religious aristocracy, it is "necessary for the historical life of the Church, for the religious educating and guidance of peoples." Berdyaev, *Inequality*, 136.

24. Berdyaev, "Concerning Anarchism," in *Inequality*, 209.

25. Berdyaev, "Anarchism," 209.

26. Ibid., 211.

27. Nikolai Berdyaev, *The New Religious Consciousness and Society* (quoted here after *Nova religijska svest i društvena stvarnost*), trans. Mirko Đorđević (Belgrade: Brimo, 2001), 201.

28. Ibid., 203.

29. See ibid., 195.

30. Berdyaev, "Anarchism," 212.

31. See Berdyaev, *The New Religious Consciousness*, 197.

32. See ibid., 211.

33. See ibid., 213.

34. Nikolai Berdyaev, *Slavery and Freedom*, trans. R.M. French (New York: Charles Scribner's Sons, 1944), 147–48. For more on Berdyaev's anarchism and his place in the history of Orthodox political theologies, see Davor Džalto, *Anarchy and the Kingdom of God: From Eschatology to Orthodox Political Theology and Back* (New York: Fordham University Press, 2021).

35. This is reflected in (Pseudo) Dionysius' remark on the purpose of "every hierarchy": "Now the assimilation to, and union with, God, as far as attainable, is deification. And this is the common goal of every Hierarchy,—the clinging love towards God and Divine things divinely and uniformly ministered; and previous to this, the complete and unswerving removal of things contrary, the knowledge of things as they are in themselves; the vision and science of sacred truth; the inspired communication of the uniform perfection of the One Itself, as far as attainable; the banquet of contemplation, nourishing intelligibly, and deifying every man elevated towards it." *Ecclesiastical Hierarchy* 1.3.

SELECT BIBLIOGRAPHY

Berdyaev, Nikolai. *The Meaning of History*. Translated by George Reavy. London: Lowe and Brydone, 1949.

——. *The New Religious Consciousness and Society*. Translated by Mirko Đorđević. Belgrade: Brimo, 2001.

——. *The Philosophy of Inequality: Letters to my Contemners, Concerning Social Philosophy*. Translated by Stephen Janos. Mohrsville, PA: Frsj Publications, 2016 [1923].

——. *Slavery and Freedom*. Translated by R.M. French. New York: Charles Scribner's Sons, 1944.

Chomsky, Noam. *On Anarchism*. London: Penguin, 2014.

Džalto, Davor. *Anarchy and the Kingdom of God: From Eschatology to Orthodox Christian Political Theology and Back*. New York: Fordham University Press, 2021.

——. *The Human Work of Art: A Theological Appraisal of Creativity and the Death of the Artist*. Yonkers, NY: SVS Press, 2014.

Gentile, Emilio. *Politics as Religion*. Translated by George Staunton. Princeton, NJ: Princeton University Press, 2006.

Lossky, Vladimir. *The Mystical Theology of the Eastern Church*. Crestwood, NY: SVS Press, 1997.

Novak, Derry. "The Place of Anarchism in the History of Political Thought." In *Patterns of Anarchy: A Collection of Writings on the Anarchist Tradition*, edited by Leonard I. Krimerman and Lewis Perry, 5–15. New York: Anchor Books, 1966.

Index

Against Eunomius (Gregory of Nyssa), 26
All We Need Is Love (Džalto), *48*
American liberalism, 120–21
anarchism. *See specific topics*
anarchist criminology, 65–68, 78n53
anarcho-bolshevism, 103, 112n6
Anarchy and Action (Ward), 66
Anderson, Benedict, 111n2
angels, 124, 129–30
annihilation, 47–51
anthropology: Christian, 40n1; Christianity in, 27–28; in political theology, 31–33; soteriology and, 34
apathy, 57
apophatic political theology, 28–32, 38
Argentina, 103, 109
aristocracy, 117, 124–30, 133n18, 133n23
ascendance, 124
ascesis, 49–51, 69–70
asceticism, 76n32, 83, 85
assimilation, 133n35
Augustine, 36–37
authority: of Jesus, 27; justice and, 67; power and, 36; in socialism, 127
Avrich, Paul, 90, 93

Bakhtin, Mikhail, 86–88

Bakunin, Michail: ideology of, 90, 92; influence of, 101, 103–5, 108, 110–11, 111n1; reputation of, 32, 127
Balthasar, Hans Uhrs von, 43n15
baptism, 9
Basil (Saint), 26, 55–57, 64–65
Beatitudes, 25
Benz, Ernst, 85
Berdyaev, Nicolai: on eschatological anarchy, 128; philosophy of, 23, 30, 40n1, 131n10, 133n23; on spiritual aristocracy, 124–27; on theocratic anarchism, 127–28
Berdyaev, Nikolai, 92
biblical scholars, 9
Blanqui, Louis Auguste, 32
Bolshevik Revolution, 103
Book of Enoch, 3–4
Books of Samuel, 7
Borges, Jorge Luis, 103
Brandes, Georg, 92
Bulgakov, Sergius, 105
burial rituals, 12–13

Caesar, 8, 12
Caesarea Philippi, 10, 17n53, 64
Camery-Hoggatt, Jerry, 4, 12
capitalism, 54–56, 72–74
Cappadocians, 35, 64

Index

Cappelletti, Angel J., 103, 105
Carcass (Pavlenskii), 95
Cartilla Socialista (Rhodokanaty), 104, 106–7
Catholicism, 65, 86, 110–11
Centuries on Love (Maximus the Confessor), 64–65
chaos, 117
Childhood (Tolstoy), 92–94
Chomsky, Noam, 59–60
Christianity: in anthropology, 27–28; capitalism and, 54–55; Cappadocians in, 64; Catholicism and, 65, 86; Christian anthropology, 40n1; churches in, 38–40; community in, 63–65; eschatology and, 122; ethics in, 58, 62, 72; freedom in, 42n31; Gnostics in, 42n31; God in, 50–51; Greek philosophy and, 71; hope in, 68–71; humanity in, 55–59, 72–73; Jesus in, 67; Judaism and, 4; Judeo-Christianity, 122–23; justice in, 35; Kingdom of God in, 39–40; to Maximus the Confessor, 47–49, *48*, 72–74, 74n9; metaphysics in, 51; monks, 86–87; Moses in, 123; nuns, 86–87; Orthodox, 87–90, 95–96, 101, *102*, 103–11; philosophy in, 23; politics of, 25, 53; in Russia, 89; sins in, 35–37; theology of, 73–74, 120; to Tolstoy, 92–94, 107–8. *See also specific topics*
Chrysostom, John, 35
churches, 23, 38–40, 108–11
Clement of Alexandria, 28, 43n46
colonialism, 112n2
El Combate, 108
communism, 119–20
community, 63–68
Constantinople, 49
Corinthians, 39
Corpus Areopagiticum, 132n13
Costa Rica, 108
COVID-19, 62
criminology, 61, 65–68, 78n53

Cuban Revolution, 104

David: in Gospel of Mark, 15n20; Jesus and, 3, 7–8; as prophet, 16n32; son of David, 3–4, 6–7, 11–12
deconstruction: deconstructive irony, 13; dramatic irony in, 1–2; in Gospel of Mark, 10n10; of justice, 30–31; reconstruction after, 3
definitions, of anarchism, 119–22, 130n3, 130n9
democracy, 31, 119–20
demon legions, 10
Déroche, Vincent, 85
Derrida, Jacques, 10n10, 42n27
Detstvo (Tolstoy), 92–94
the Devil, 36, 39–40
disaster relief, 60–62
Dostoevsky, Fedor, 85–86
dramatic irony, 1–2, 4–6
Džalto, Davor. *See specific topics*

Eastern Orthodox churches, 23
Ecclesiastes, 25, 35–36
economics: capitalism, 54–55; ethics and, 62–63; ideology and, 91; politics and, 57–58
Edict of Milan, 25
empty tomb, 12–13
Enlightenment rationalism, 105
epektasis, 68
eschatological anarchy, 128
eschatological immanence, 73
eschatological superhuman, 4
eschatology, 34, 38–40, 69–70, 75n17, 122
ethics: of capitalism, 54–56; in Christianity, 58, 62, 72; economics and, 62–63; humanity and, 52; of Maximus the Confessor, 55–58; theology and, 65–66; virtue, 35, 52–53, 70–71, 76n23
etymology, 117
Europe, 106, 108–10
European Imperialism, 107

Index 137

European rationalism, 85–86
evangelical theology, 42n39
evil hierarchies, 122
evil time, 131n10
exile, 26
exorcism, 9–10, 16n29
An Experiment in Eschatological Metaphysics (Džalto), *102*
exploitation, 58–59

faith, 12–13, 40
false prophets, 110
false time, 131n10
federation, 63–65
Ferrel, Jeff, 66–67, 71
First International, 103
Fixation (Pavlenskii), 95
Florenskii, Pavel, 88
A Fool for Christ (Xenia of St. Petersburg) (Džalto), *84*
Foucault, Michel, 89
Fourier, Charles, 66, 106
freedom: anthropology and, 31–33; in apophatic political theology, 38; in Christianity, 42n31; free expression, 60; humanity and, 25–26; rational, 36; spiritual "nomadism" and, 96
"Free Socialism," 106
Froelich, Margaret, 10

Garcia Monge, Joaquim, 113n24
Germany, 105–6
global capitalism, 55–56
Gnostics, 42n31
God. *See specific topics*
Goldman, Emma, 76n80
Gomes, Carlos, 103
Gonzalez Prada, Manuel, 104
Gospel of Mark: David in, 15n20; deconstruction in, 14n10; dramatic irony in, 6; empty tomb in, 12–13; irony in, 4; Israel in, 14n9; Jerusalem in, 16n33; Jesus in, 6–8, 18n57; Judaism and, 4–5; messianic language in, 1, *2*, 3, 5; messianic

secret in, 15n17; narrators in, 15n18; Psalms and, 16n25; readers of, 15n16; Rome in, 8–11; royal messianic language in, 11–12, 15n19; scholarship on, 14n11, 17n40; Superscription, 6
Greek language, 41n10
Greek Orthodoxy, 110–11
Greek philosophy, 71
Gregory of Nazianzus (Saint), 64, 132n12
Gregory of Nyssa (Saint): Balthasar on, 41n15; freedom to, 31–33, 42n31; on Greek language, 41n10; justice to, 30–31; on love, 67–68; love of rule to, 36–37; Macrina the Younger and, 42n34; on materialism, 55; peacemaking to, 37–38; philosophy of, 64–65, 69; political theology of, 23, *24*, 25–26, 28–32; on power, 38–40; Ramilli on, 43n52; on slavery, 33–37; on subordinationism, 26–28
Guerrero, Praxedis, 104

Hart, David Bentley, 38
healer/saviors, 7, 9–10
"Heilige Narrheit" Benz, Ernst, 85
A Hierarch on Fire (Džalto), *116*
hierarchy, 115, *116*, 117–19, 122–30
Hinkelammert, Franz, 104
historical aristocracy, 125
History of Madness (Foucault), 89
Hobbes, Thomas, 58
holy fools: as anarchism, 83, *84*, 85, 90–92; in literature, 92–94; in Russia, 94–97; in scholarship, 85–89
hope, 68–71
humanity: in Christianity, 55–59, 72–73; the Devil to, 39–40; eschatology and, 69–70; ethics and, 52; freedom and, 25–26; God and, 28–29; human essence, 42n34; human nature, 50; human relations, 27–28, 37; human rights, 120–21; as image of God,

30–32; inequality in, 30–31; of Jesus, 42n39, 68, 71; Kingdom of God and, 122; love and, 109–10; Maximus the Confessor on, 75n13, 75n18; in natural disasters, 61–62; ontology of, 32; philosophy of, 33–34, 49–50; power and, 26–27; scholarship on, 75n14; status quo in, 59–63; virtue ethics and, 70–71
humility, 31–33, 37–38
Hurricane Harvey, 61

Iangulova, Liia, 88–89
ideology: of anarchism, 79n80; of Bakunin, 90, 92; conformity to, 118–19; economics and, 91; ideological narratives, 117–18; political, 59–60; politics and, 5; royal, 3–4, 7; of symphonia, 59–60
imperial ideology, 4, 9
imperial language, 9
imperial vocabulary, 8, 10–11
impossibility, 58–59
inequality, 30–31, 68–69
irony. *See specific topics*
Isaac, 67–68
Isaiah, 11
Islam, 110
Israel, 14n9
iurodstvo, 83, 85–86, 88–97
"I Will Tear Down My Barns" (Basil), 64

Jerusalem: destruction of, 9; in Gospel of Mark, 16n33; Jesus in, 7–8, 10–11; Psalms, 6–7; royal ideology in, 3–4; Temple of Jerusalem, 123–24
Jesus: angels and, 129–30; in art, 95; authority of, 27; baptism of, 9; in Christianity, 67; David and, 3, 7–8; depictions of, 2; as *eschatological superhuman*, 4; as exorcist, 16n29; in Gospel of Mark, 6–8, 18n57; holy foolishness of, 86–89, 92–93;

humanity of, 42n39, 68, 71; identity of, 5–8; interpretations of, 13; *iurodstvo* and, 83; in Jerusalem, 7–8, 10–11; as Kingdom of God, 31, 129; messianic language and, 14n2, 15n19; to Paul, 56, 83, 85, 89; Peter and, 5; philosophy of, 54, 57; Pilate and, 11–12, 18n59; politics of, 1–2; in Rome, 56; son of David and, 6, 12; Spirit of God and, 6–7; in trinity theology, 31–33
John of Damascus (Saint), 73
Joseph, 10, 17n53
Judaism: Book of Enoch in, 3–4; Caesar in, 8; Christianity and, 4; Gospel of Mark and, 4–5; King of the Jews, 12; scriptural language in, 3–4
Judeo-Christianity, 122–23
Jung Mo Sung, 104
justice: authority and, 67; Derrida on, 42n27; in Lord's Prayer, 34–35; mercy and, 67–68; political theology of, 30–31; popular, 66
Justin Martyr, 28

Kant, Immanuel, 26
Kingdom of God: as anarchy, 128; in Christianity, 39–40; humanity and, 122; humility and, 32–33; Jesus as, 31, 129; sacrifices to, 126; scholarship on, 29–30
The King Who Would Not Be King (Džalto), 2
Kovalevskii, Ioann, 85
Kropotkin, Pyotr, 60–64, 67–71, 90, 92, 101, 111n1
Kuznetsov, Aleksei, 85

Latin America: anarchism in, 112n5; anarcho-bolshevism in, 112n6; churches in, 109–10; colonialism in, 111n2; literature in, 113n24; Orthodox Christianity in, 101, *102*, 103–11; Russia and, 101, 103, 112n15

Index 139

Law and Authority (Kropotkin), 69
legions, of demons, 10
Le Guin, Ursula, 73–74
Lenin, Vladimir, 94, 103
liberal democracies, 118
liberalism, 120–21, 130n9
Likhachev, Dmitrii, 86, 90, 95
lineages, 15n20
literature, 85–89, 92–94, 107–8, 113n24
Llaguno Thomas, José Julian, 108, 113n24
logoi, 50–53, 55, 71, 74n10
Lopez, Julio, 106
Lord's Prayer, 34–35
Lossky, Vladimir, 132n12
love: annihilation and, 47–51; as God, 70–71; Gregory of Nyssa on, 67–68; humanity and, 109–10; of rule, 36–37; self-love and, 52–55, 62
Luther, Martin, 86

Macrina the Younger the Younger (Saint), 32, 42n34
Magon, Flores, 104
Malatesta, Errico, 66, 101, 130n4
Mandelstam, Osip, 91–92
Mariátegui, José, 104
Mark. *See* Gospel of Mark
Martinez Andrade, Luis, 112n5
Marxism, 90, 101, 104, 108
materialism, 55
Matthew, 95
Maximus the Confessor (Saint): anarchist criminology and, 65–68; Christianity to, 47–49, *48*, 72–74, 74n9; ethics of, 55–58; on humanity, 75n13, 75n18; on *logoi*, 74n10; metaphysics of, 68–71; property to, 63–65; reputation of, 74n2; on self-love, 52–55; theology of, 58–59; theory of spontaneous order to, 59–63; theosis to, 49–51; virtue ethics of, 76n23
Memoirs of a Revolutionist (Kropotkin), 92

mercy, 67–68
messianic language: faith and, 12–13; in Gospel of Mark, 1, *2*, 3, 5; imperial vocabulary and, 10–11; interpretations of, 18n61; Jesus and, 14n2, 15n19; lineages in, 15n20; messianic secret, 15n17; royal, 11–12, 15n19; scholarship on, 3–11; son of David in, 7, 11
metaphysics: art and, *102*; in Christianity, 51; of Maximus the Confessor, 68–71; theology and, 57–58
Mexico, 103–6, 108–9, 111
Miliukov, Pael, 94
Mirbeau, Octave, 117
Mistral, Gabriel, 113n24
mock processions, 18n60
mock trials, 18n57
modernity, 54–55
monks, 86–87
Moore, Stephen D., 14n10
Moses, 123, 131n11, 132n12
Mutual Aid (Kropotkin), 70
mystical ascension, 122–23
The Mystical Theology of the Eastern Church (Lossky), 132n12

natural disasters, 60–62
nature, 77n17
necessity, 58–59, 70
negative political theology, 29
neustra America, 103
Nicene doctrine, 25–26
Nietzsche, Friedrich, 92
Not by Violence (Džalto), *24*
Novak, Derry, 130n9
Nulia, Enrique, 113n24
nuns, 86–87

On the Making of Man (Gregory of Nyssa), 32
On the Soul and the Resurrection (Marcrina), 32
ontology, 32

140 *Index*

oppression, 117–21, 126–28, 131
Orthodox asceticism, 83, 85
Orthodox Christianity, 87–90, 95–96, 101, *102*, 103–11
orthodoxy. *See specific topics*
Our Lord's Prayer, 29
Owen, Robert, 106

Panchenko, Aleksandr, 86, 90, 95
Pantiukhov, Ivan, 92
Patterns of Anarchy (Novak), 130n9
Paul, 39, 56, 83, 85, 89
Pavlenskii, Piotr, 94–97
Pax Romana, 8
peacemaking, 37–38
Perovskaya, Sophia, 92
Peru, 103
Peter, 5
Peter the Great, 89
philosophy: of anarchism, 71; of Berdyaev, 23, 30, 40n1, 131n10, 133n23; in Christianity, 23; of faith, 40; Greek, 71; of Gregory of Nyssa, 64–65, 69; of humanity, 33–34, 49–50; of Isaiah, 11; of Jesus, 54, 57; literature and, 85–89; political, 127; of property, 63–64; from Russia, 92, 96–97; theology and, 59, 64–65; of trinity, 25–28; of true religion, 109
Pilate, 11–12, 18n59
Pioneer Health Centre, 60
Platonov, Andrei, 94, 96
political ideology, 59–60
political philosophy, 127
political power, 37–38, 40
political systems, 117
political theology: anthropology in, 31–33; apophatic, 28–32, 38; eschatology and, 38–40; of Gregory of Nyssa, 23, *24*, 25–26, 28–32; of humility, 37–38; of justice, 30–31; negative, 29; power in, 36–37; of property, 34–36; subordinationism in, 26–28

politics: of Chomsky, 59–60; of Christianity, 25, 53; economics and, 57–58; ideology and, 5; of Jesus, 1–2; of oppression, 117–21, 126–28, 131
popular justice, 66
power: authority and, 36; Berdyaev on, 30; in capitalism, 72–74; in Ecclesiastes, 35–36; of exploitation, 59; Gregory of Nyssa on, 38–40; humanity and, 26–27; inequality and, 68–69; oppression and, 126; political, 37–38; in political theology, 36–37; pyramid of, 128–29; scholarship on, 26; structures, 117–18; of violence, 68–69
pride, 36
progressivism, 120–21
property, 34–36, 63–65
prophets, 7, 16n32
Protestantism, 23, 110–11
proto-anarchism, 107
Proudhon, Pierre Joseph, 101, 103, 105–6, 127
Psalms, 3, 6–7, 16n25
public opinion, 119–20
Pussy Riot, 94–97
Putin, Vladimir, 94
pyramid of power, 128–29

Ramilli, Ilaria, 43n52
Rasputin, 89
rational freedom, 36
readers: dramatic irony for, 4–5; empty tomb to, 13; of Gospel of Mark, 15n16; imperial language for, 9; in Rome, 10
Read & Riot (Tolokonnikova), 94–95
Rebel Zapatista Autonomous Municipalities, 65
reconstruction, 3
refugees, 121
Rhodokanaty, Plotino, 104–11, 112n15
Roman Catholicism, 23, 26, 105, 110–11

Rome: Constantinople and, 49; in Gospel of Mark, 8–11; imperial ideology in, 4; Jesus in, 56; mock processions in, 18n60; *Pax Romana*, 8; readers in, 10; royal ideology in, 3
royal ideology, 3–4, 7
royal messianic language, 11–12, 15n19
Russia: anarcho-bolshevism, 103, 112n6; Bolshevik Revolution, 103; culture of, 83, *84*, 85, 88–97; Latin America and, 101, 103, 112n15; scholarship on, 90, 94; tsarism in, 105. *See also iurodstvo*
The Russian Anarchists (Avrich), 90
Rydén, Lennart, 85

Sanhedrin, 18n58
scriptural language, 3–4
Seam (Pavlenskii), 95
Second Temple period, 3, 4
Segundo, Juan Luis, 104
self-destruction, 57
self-love, 52–55, 62
Semero sviatykh (Ulitskaia), 89
Shestov, Lev, 85–86
sin, 35–37
slavery, 33–37, 39
Smekh v Drevnei Rusi (Panchenko and Likhachev), 86
La Social, 106
social conformity, 118–19
socialism, 103–11, 127
El Socialista (journal), 107
Sola fide doctrine, 86
Soloviev, Vladimir, 112n15
Song of Songs, 32, 39–40
son of David, 3–4, 6–7, 11–12
soteriology, 34
Soviet Union, 89, 130n9
Spirit of God, 6–7
spiritual aristocracy, 124–27, 128–30
spiritual "nomadism," 96
status quo, 59–63, 118–19
Stierner, Max, 127
Stockholm University, 91

subordinationism, 26–28, 42n39
symphonia, 59–60

Temple of Jerusalem, 123–24
Tent/Temples, 123–24
theocratic anarchism, 127–30
theology: apophatic political, 28–32, 38; of Christianity, 73–74, 120; ethics and, 65–66; evangelical, 42n39; exploitation in, 58; history of, 47–49; of Maximus the Confessor, 58–59; metaphysics and, 57–58; philosophy and, 59, 64–65; trinity, 25–28, 31–33. *See also* political theology
theory of spontaneous order, 59–63
theosis, 49–51, 69–70
Thompson, Ewa, 85
"The Threat" (Pavlenskii), 95
time, 131n10
Tollefsen, T., 75n14
Tolokonnikova, Nadezhda, 94–95
Tolstoy, Lev: anarchism and, 107–8, 113n24; influence of, 85–86, 92–94, 96; Proudhon and, 127
"Tolstoy as the Mirror of the Russian Revolution" (Lenin), 94
transfiguration, 124
translations, 15n14
trinity theology, 25–28, 31–33
Tristan, Flora, 104
tropos, 50–52
The True Church, 108–11
true religion, 109

Ulitskaia, Ludmila, 89
(un)holy hierarchies, 122–28
United States, 61

Valades, José C., 106
Valens (emperor), 25
Vallverde y Telles (bishop), 105
Van Steenwyk, Mark, 30
Vespasian, 9
violence, 68–69
virtue ethics, 35, 52–53, 70–71, 76n23

142 *Index*

Ward, Colin, 60–62, 66
Winn, Adam, 9–10
women, 12–13

Yananras, Christos, 105

Zamyatin, Yevgeny, 121–22
Zapata, Emiliano, 104
Zhelyabov, Andrei, 92

About the Contributors

Veljko Birač is a teacher of Biblical studies at Sankt Ignatios College in Sweden. He received a master's degree in Biblical studies from the Faculty of Orthodox Theology, University of Belgrade in Serbia. His research focuses on messianism within the ancient Judaistic literary corpus.

Per-Arne Bodin is professor of Slavic languages at Stockholm University. He has written extensively on Russian, Polish, and Ukrainian literatures, as well as on the relation between Russian culture and Orthodox tradition. He is a member of the Royal Swedish Academy of Letters, History, and Antiquities and doctor honoris causa at Uppsala University. His most recent books are *Eternity and Time: Studies in Russian Literature and the Orthodox Tradition* (2007) and *Language, Canonization and Holy Foolishness: Studies in Post-Soviet Russian Culture and the Orthodox Tradition* (2009).

E. Brown Dewhurst is an independent scholar, author, and poet based in Scotland. He received his doctoral degree from Durham University and completed his postdoctoral research at Ludwig Maximilians Universität in Munich on Maximus the Confessor and Gregory of Nyssa. His main research interests are in patristic theology, ethics, and anarchism.

Davor Džalto is professor in religion and democracy at University College Stockholm. He is also president of the Institute for the Study of Culture and Christianity. His research focuses primarily on the exploration of human freedom and creativity, as metaphysical, political, as well as aesthetic concepts. His most recent books are: *Beyond Capitalist Dystopia* (2022) and *Anarchy and the Kingdom of God* (2021). As a practicing artist, he works primarily in the medium of painting.

Graham McGeoch is a theologian and minster of the Church of Scotland. He received his PhD in theology and religious studies from the University of Glasgow. He is associate professor of theology and religious studies at Faculdade Unida de Vitória in Brazil, and a mission secretary to the Council for World Mission.

Johannes A. Steenbuch received his PhD in philosophy and theology from the University of Copenhagen with a dissertation on negative theology and ethics in Clement of Alexandria and Gregory of Nyssa. He is the editor of *Tidsskriftet Fønix* and secretary of the Danish Patristics Society. His most recent book is *Negative Theology: A Short Introduction* (2022).